NO LESSONS LEARNED

VIETNAM: THE FIGHTING, THE DYING,
A LEGACY REPLAYED IN THE MIDDLE EAST

ALFREDO BONADEO

Copyright © 2023 Alfredo Bonadeo.

All rights reserved. No part of this book may be reproduced, stored, or transmitted by any means—whether auditory, graphic, mechanical, or electronic—without written permission of both publisher and author, except in the case of brief excerpts used in critical articles and reviews. Unauthorized reproduction of any part of this work is illegal and is punishable by law.

ISBN: 979-8-88640-352-7 (sc)
ISBN: 979-8-88640-353-4 (hc)
ISBN: 979-8-88640-355-8 (e)

Because of the dynamic nature of the Internet, any web addresses or links contained in this book may have changed since publication and may no longer be valid. The views expressed in this work are solely those of the author and do not necessarily reflect the views of the publisher, and the publisher hereby disclaims any responsibility for them.

One Galleria Blvd., Suite 1900, Metairie, LA 70001
1-888-421-2397

CONTENTS

Acknowledgments v
Introduction vii

Chapter 1 – Due Cause 1
    A War Without a Cause 1

Chapter 2 – The Killing 25
    Victims to Abusers 25
    Under Fire 33
    Psychotic Breakdown or Going Berserk 35
    Weaponry 39
    The Invisible Enemy 41
    Body Count 45
    My Lai 48
    Survival 51
    The Making of Heroes 52
    Training 55
    The Man I Killed 57

Chapter 3 – The Dying 59
    Hiding the Truth 59
    Ghosts 62
    The Pervasiveness of Death 63
    The Environment 64
    Death's Ravages 65
    Fear 68
    Fatalism 71
    Combat Assault 73
    Search and Destroy 76

    Sacrifice 79
    Courage 81
    Due Cause 83
    Proving One's Manhood 84
    Altered States of Being 86
    Waste 90
    What Remains 92
    Survival 95
    Why Veterans Miss War 97

Chapter 4 – The Legacy 99
    New Wars 103
    Broken Lives 109
    Moral Burden 112
    War Changes a Man's Nature 114
    Conventional War vs Asymmetrical War 115
    Heroism and the Heroic Ideal 117
    War and the Soul 120

Conclusion 125
Epilogue 131
    Hiding the Truth 132
Endnotes 135
Index 148

ACKNOWLEDGMENTS

I would like to express my thanks to those who have helped me finish this book after the death of Alfredo Bonadeo. First to Professor Harry Lawton, a friend and colleague of my husband who wrote the introduction and helped with the editing of the manuscript, to John Weber who provided source material for many of the events in the Middle East that occurred after June 2011, to my daughter, Sabrina Bell-Bonadeo, for her help with my struggle to understand the Microsoft formatting, and finally, to those writers and critics many of whom I have extensively quoted in this work, for their impassioned voices in bringing to the forefront, the human and societal cost of an American foreign policy that has, since World War II become increasingly militarily driven.

Barbara Bates Bonadeo

INTRODUCTION

When Alfredo Bonadeo died in June 2011, he left behind an unfinished manuscript on the Vietnam war. His wife, Barbara, edited and wrote the final chapter and the epilogue to complete it and bring it current with the times. Bonadeo's work did not appear out of the blue. For the previous thirty- five years he had returned on four occasions to the theme of war and its consequences. The main body of these prior studies focuses on the soldier's experience in World War I. That military holocaust continues to serve as the ill-begotten model for all the wars and military tragedies in the twentieth century that followed: the industrialization of warfare and its global reach, the mass conscription of nations, the wholesale slaughter of soldiers and civilians alike, the destruction of towns and cities, the sacrifice of generations, and, even more insidious, the militarization of economies. The war to end all wars was in fact the matrix or incubator of the 20th-century wars to come, building on the mass destruction of its predecessor. It nurtured the poisonous germs that erupted a scant twenty years later in the second World War. Two European dictators served in the trenches of World War I, and that experience planted the seeds that nurtured the toxic doctrines of Fascism and Nazism that engulfed Europe and the world in the decades to come.

Bonadeo was acquainted with war. Born in the town of Volpedo in Piedmont, he was 12 when Mussolini dragged Italy into World War II on the side of the Axis, and 17 when the war ended. He would have learned of the fate of thousands of fellow Piedmontese, a few years older than he, drafted into the Alpini and sent to die in the snows of Russia, leaving widows, children, and devastated families behind. He would have been aware of the guerilla war raging in the region between the Fascist defenders of the rump Social Republic of Mussolini (centered in Salo) and the resistance forces arrayed against the Fascists and retreating Germans. He would certainly have seen and heard the allied planes flying overhead on bombing runs to and from Turin and Milan, not that far distant from Volpedo. And the battlegrounds of World War I, along with preserved trenches, were not that far away further east in Friuli and Venezia Giulia, where Italian and Austrian forces faced off in the snows of the Dolomites. Certainly, all these memories, personal, historical, and geographical, will have left an impression.

Coming from an Italian professor of literature, these war studies understandably proceed along closely related tracks. There is an emphasis (but not exclusive) on the Italian experience in World War I, along with an understanding of the value of literature in conveying the feelings and viewpoints of serving soldiers enduring the daily business of war. Italian conservatives like Benedetto Croce and rabid nationalists like Giovanni Papini—extensively quoted in Bonadeo's *Mark of the Beast* (1975)—were passionate interventionists. For them, as for the futurist leader Marinetti who stated that "war is the only hygiene of the world," war alone would redeem the country from the decadent torpor into which it had slumped since the struggle for unity and independence in the Risorgimento half a century earlier.

For Gabriele D'Annunzio, the poet who won considerable renown for himself as a warrior (and the subject of Bonadeo's second book on this period), the war was an opportunity for personal redemption by way of heroic risk, a baptism in blood. This national hero showed remarkably little understanding of the national and international issues at stake, of the strategic value of the operations he undertook, and even less appreciation of the futile sacrifice of hundreds and thousands of ordinary soldiers from the lower ranks of society. In fact, in The *Mark of The Beast,* most of the writers quoted applauded the opportunity for a bloody purge of a slumbering, but potentially dangerous, the proletariat. Such sentiments, the author notes, did not augur well for Italy in the post-war era.

In the Anglo-Saxon experience, Bonadeo found a far more conscience-stricken assessment of war and its consequences. Doubtless, many writers accepted the call-up and went to war in a spirit of patriotic enthusiasm, only later to feel and express horror at the seemingly endless sacrifice of a generation of compatriots. Most emblematic of this passage from youthful idealism to dark disillusion was the poet and memoirist Siegfried Sassoon, who became a major writer tempered by the fires of war. In spite of the fact that he wrote an open letter to parliament denouncing the war and its handling, he returned to the front lines in solidarity with his men.

T.E. Lawrence (Lawrence of Arabia and the author of *The Seven Pillars of Wisdom*), fighting in a very different theatre, plays a central role in *The Mark of The Beast*. He offers Bonadeo an example of a civilized man who found he enjoyed warfare and the thrill of killing the enemy. It horrified him that war released in him an excitement that came from the exercise of violence. It was this very horror that led Lawrence later to resign his commission and re-enlist in the air force under an assumed name, seeking in anonymity a penance for his earlier behavior.

D'Annunzio and The Great War (1995) grows directly out of *The Mark of The Beast* and is exclusively a study of the poet's role in exhorting his countrymen to enter the war, and thus by virtue of that commitment, to sacrifice any number of lives in the name of national glory. That D'Annunzio was a dedicated warmonger is a given, but Bonadeo makes it clear that war for him was a personal quest, not a nationalist cause. In a string of pre-war novels,[1] he rigorously tracked a series of tumultuous love affairs, all of which ended in the protagonist's dissatisfaction and a profound feeling of self-loathing. In the final analysis, the writer's tireless search for transcendence via the bodily embrace only left him with a sense of emptiness. That exhaustion of flesh and spirit might have been expected in a man who was fifty- two years old when Italy entered the war in May 1915. But for D'Annunzio war alone, with its promise of adventure, heroic risk and a daily duel with death offered what he saw as a chance for personal resurrection.

It is quite extraordinary that D'Annunzio should conceive that World War I (or any war) was for him, a stage on which he could dramatize his daring. But that was indeed the case, and Bonadeo chronicles his exploits in great detail. In the context of a conflict involving hundreds and thousands of men, organized in whole divisions, brigades, and battalions, rendered virtually anonymous in their drab military uniforms, a self-promoter like D'Annunzio could hardly be expected to melt away into anonymity. His desire to participate in the war was welcomed by the highest military authorities, in particular general Luigi Cadorna, made notorious later as the loser of Caporetto (1917. D'Annunzio was granted all sorts of privileges: immediate elevation as an officer in the cavalry, the use of his car, a driver put at his disposal, and a personal pilot for his propaganda flights over Trieste, Trento, and Vienna. The military establishment assumed D'Annunzio would be a bystander, a spectator of the war, and a chronicler who would publicize the heroic achievements of the generals and their troops. But the poet, of course, rejected that passive role and threw himself into battle (or at least close to it). He witnessed the battle for the Carso, in which Italian soldiers threw themselves suicidally against an impregnable rock wall and Austrian barbed wire, to be mown down by withering enemy machine gun fire. While others were aghast at this useless slaughter of thousands of men, without any gain of ground, D'Annunzio saluted the wholesale spilling of blood as a necessary and worthy national sacrifice.

No one could deny his physical courage, as he took to sea and air in an unquenchable search for glory and a ceaseless challenge to death itself in several extremely risky missions, many of which involved the delivery of propaganda flyers, urging Austrian citizens to abandon the war. But as Bonadeo and all who have followed his career, think back on these reckless flights over enemy territory and commando raids by sea, it is hard not to question their strategic value.

When combat finally ended, D'Annunzio persuaded himself that he simply could not live without war. It had become a narcotic on which he depended. For him, the only solution was to deny the armistice of 1918 and continue the conflict on his terms, and he was easily persuaded to lead the march on the port of Fiume following the war's end and claim it in the name of the Italian state. That same state, of course, had already accepted the terms of the peace treaty which granted Dalmatia to the Yugoslavian authorities. Again, it was not national pride, nor a political lust for territorial acquisition, that led him to occupy Fiume. It was no more than the illusion that this very act of defiance and challenge to international law would restore in him the heroic virility he exhibited in his wartime exploits. Here, in almost parodic form, was a re-assertion of the twisted version of the superman doctrine he had elaborated in his pre-war literary works, notably *Le vergini delle rocce* (*The Maidens of the Rocks*) in which he envisioned a world governed by the superior beings of a master race. The whole Fiume episode exists in juxtaposition to the quite palpable sense of encroaching old age, and the weakening of his body and spirit.

The focus on D'Annunzio is most pertinent to Bonadeo's extended inquiry into the nature of warfare, the minds of those who plan and fight the wars, and the psychological toll on combatants and society. D'Annunzio embodies to an extreme degree the perverse conjunction of manly virility and a popular form of heroism while personifying a dangerous element in the Italian character, not at all uncommon in the period in which he was writing. That element is a taste for violence and a belief that Italy needed a wholesale sacrifice of flesh and blood to claim a respected place among nations. This, need to recapture the greatness of its Roman past, combined with a visceral contempt for the peasant and working classes who comprised almost all the rank and file of the soldiers who flung themselves futilely against the Austrian machine guns on the Carso and the banks of the Isonzo, was designed to appease the military demand for blood and sacrifice. One may see how out of the seeds of extreme nationalist dogma would grow the doctrine and political foundation of fascism.

Someone else drew similar lessons from participation in the Great War. Benito Mussolini served dutifully, if not spectacularly, on the Austrian front in the infantry, eventually reaching the rank of sergeant, from September 1915 until June 1917, when he was invalided out as a result of wounds from a grenade launcher during a training exercise. The future dictator of Italy is the subject of Bonadeo's third study of the motivations of those who go to war, and whose ideology is formed from it. The book is *Mussolini and the Politics of Sacrifice*[2] written in Italian and published in Italy. Mussolini had been a revolutionary socialist as late as August 1914, at which point he made a one-hundred-eighty-degree turn, abruptly leaving the Socialist party, resigning his position as editor of the party paper, Avanti, and opportunistically declaring himself an ardent interventionist.

Like all other proponents of nationalist doctrine, Mussolini convinced himself that Italians in general, and the working class in particular, including the peasantry, were weak, apathetic, morally indifferent, and totally lacking in patriotic fervor. What was needed, therefore, to ensure the country's national resurgence, was a baptism in blood, an exposure to the realities of mechanized warfare. This, he believed, would make the survivors stronger and better Italians. Furthermore, the imposition of an iron military discipline would render them more compliant with the authority of their superiors, in civilian as well as military life. Sacrifice, in short, was the key to national redemption.

There was a rather obvious difference between Mussolini and D'Annunzio. The latter only measured the war and its aftermath in terms of personal sublimation (something he never actually achieved). Mussolini was a political animal, for whom the cult of violence, endemic to warfare, was something he could transform into political doctrine. This in turn was to be imposed on those he assumed to be his docile compatriots. Quoting liberally from Mussolini's war diaries, his post-war speeches, which would later be incorporated into the later official doctrine of fascism, Bonadeo reveals a sinister similarity between the vocabulary of many of D'Annunzio's more outrageous calls for war, his verbal assaults on neutralist politicians, and that of Mussolini who embraced, at least linguistically, the concepts of violence and redemptive death. It is worth noting, however, that Mussolini managed to avoid participation in a number of assaults on the enemy. At the same time, he frequently boasted of his own propensity to violence as a schoolboy, and his readiness to use it in later years, both to suppress opposition and even eliminate opponents.

Even as a simple lieutenant during the war, Mussolini fully endorsed the policy of brutal discipline imposed by the Italian High Command, and in particular by General Cadorna, head of the Army, on the ordinary soldiers. This policy demanded absolute obedience to every order, no matter how nonsensical in some circumstances, and tolerated not the slightest murmur of dissent. Cadorna imposed an essentially despotic discipline on his troops, whom he plainly despised. The very hint, let alone open expression, of dissent, was met with the harshest punishment, often immediate execution and even decimation. His unwavering belief in human waves of assault, mindless of the armed strength of the enemy, protected by their fortified bunkers, led to the devastating defeat at Caporetto in 1917.

Mussolini noted with approval how the application of brutal discipline by the commanders resulted in their absolute control over the soldiers under their command, men who knew that as they rose from the trenches, they were marching to their death; and yet they went, and never rebelled. He concluded that if such control was possible in times of war, why not in the political arena in times of peace? He shared D'Annunzio's contempt for the ordinary citizen whose main characteristic was passive stoicism and a resignation to his fate. Here was the raw material that a despotic leader could bend to his will. The imposition of discipline and unquestioning obedience through fear was the model he would apply to Italian political life in the two decades following World War I.

Through violence and intimidation, the fascist regime in the 1920s attempted to silence all serious opposition. Hence the incarceration of the Communist Party leadership on trumped-up charges in 1926. Hence the phenomenon of "squadrismo", sending thugs into the street to beat up anyone suspected of anti-fascist views or activity, along with assaults on Socialist Party offices, and the destruction of their printing presses. Hence the assault and murder of prominent critics of the regime who continued to speak out against its most egregious crimes: Giacomo Matteotti (1924), and Giovanni Amendola (1925). In painstaking detail, Bonadeo illustrates the hardening of central fascist principles in the trenches of World War I.

His penultimate study of men at war is *Martial Valor from Beowulf to Vietnam* (2010). This is essentially a literary history of warfare. The author proceeds chronologically from *Beowulf* to *The Song of Roland*, through Shakespeare (mostly the histories), Tasso's *Jerusalem Delivered*, Stephen Crane's, *The Red Badge of Courage*, Tolstoy's *War and Peace*, on into the literature of the first and second World Wars, ending with a lengthy final chapter on Vietnam. The latter amounts to an introduction to the current volume. While the books quoted in that chapter do not amount to major works of literature, they do serve as a direct record of the experience of the troops who fought and died there, enshrined in a variety of forms, including memoirs, fiction, and some fine journalism. Throughout this study, the author employs what may be regarded as the military vocabulary of glory, words like valor, courage, sacrifice, and hero, and he debates—or lets his authors debate—their precise meaning. It is clear that these words have, through the press of circumstances, been drained of meaning in our own time. Where once such vocabulary embodied an indisputable nobility and unquestioned virtue, in a world that has witnessed universal carnage, state-sponsored genocide, and a litter of broken promises, it now rings hollow with the echo of empty rhetoric.

In his book on Machiavelli,[3] Bonadeo's choice of the word "valor," conform to the Secretary's use of the term "virtu". In, *The Prince* and other works, this is strictly a military term. It refers to physical courage, determination to eliminate an enemy, an acceptance of, even a relish for, violence, and the ruthless determination of the leader. It designates the behavior of the soldier on the battlefield and is the measure of the warrior. In past centuries, no one questioned the status of a hero's "virtu" nor the evident destructiveness of his actions. Indeed, the more deaths he inflicted, the greater his renown. Whether he fought for personal glory (*Beowulf*), God and King (*Roland*, and his literary descendants such as Orlando, or Rinaldo and the crusading knights in the *Jerusalem Delivered*, or to prove himself a king (Shakespeare's *Henry V*), it was understood that the hero was a superior being. He always stood and fought at the apex of the feudal hierarchy. He never emerged from the ranks. No one—least of all himself—reflected on the consequences of his actions.

A reading of *Martial Valor* reveals that only in the more broadly educated, and therefore skeptical, Twentieth Century—starting with the wholesale slaughter in World War I—would the voice of the ordinary soldier be raised and heard, and with it the questioning, even the downright rejection, of those ancient values, which have lost their luster in the context of industrialized warfare. The process begins in the slowly democratizing nineteenth century when we first hear the voice of the private, as in the case of Henry Fleming, the protagonist of Stephen Crane's *The Red Badge of Courage*. Henry never examines the reasons for the war. Attracted by the false lure of the uniform and the martial music, he joins up. Overwhelmed by fear, he first deserts the field of battle. He returns, and only later, at the sight of death's ravages on one of his comrades, acquires the will to fight. The tragic irony is that it is not through human compassion, but fear of his own death and horror at its assault on the body that arouses his fighting spirit. The courage that he finally exhibits is divorced from ultimate moral courage, which comes from genuine regard for others.

A skeptical and more democratic voice increases in volume as Bonadeo examines the literature of the twentieth century's two world wars. In part, this is territory already examined in *The Mark of The Beast*. We hear a change in tone in the vocabulary of the poets who came of age in the Great War. The language of writers like Siegfried Sassoon, Wilfred Owen, Robert Graves, and Isaac Rosenberg directly reflects the brutalities and waste of war, marking a complete break with the softer sentimentality of Edwardian verse, more accurately represented by such poets as Rupert Brooke. A similar abrasive tone is apparent in the prose of T.E Lawrence, whose *Seven Pillars of Wisdom* includes the author's disavowal of his own military prowess, which he ultimately conceived as sanctioned barbarism.

Bonadeo's examples show the voice of the ordinary soldier growing louder as we move through the war literature of the 20th century. The image of the warrior cast in an allegedly heroic mold is turned on its head in examples of American fiction coming out of World War II. In Norman Mailer's *The Naked and The Dead*, men waiting to fight the Japanese the following day feel nothing but fear. That is their enemy, and the code of the time requires that they do everything not to show it. Only one of their companies approximates the standard image of the hero, Sergeant Croft, and that is because he is a natural-born killer. Croft has a great capacity for hate, and it is that which provides his armor in battle. Mailer's book was published shortly after the war in which he served, and the experience was fresh in his memory. Joseph Heller's *Catch 22* was written nearly twenty years after the war and reflects that cultural detachment. In Yossarian, Heller created the perfect anti-hero for what would be a rebellious decade. As a navigator in a bomber over Italy, Yossarian's approach to war is to avoid action at all costs. Ultimately his goal is not just to survive, but to desert. He sets his mind on neutral Sweden. (Was not that also the goal of many draft resisters and military deserters in the Vietnam period?) In

Yossarian's final flight we catch a glimpse of the eponymous protagonist of Tim O'Brien's novel, *Going After Cacciato*.

The final chapter of *Martial Valor* is devoted to the literature of Vietnam and is the origin of the volume that follows. It offers the sharpest contradiction to the historical embrace of the warrior hero, stretching from Homer to the Renaissance. As the war dragged on, and the American military presence swelled to over half a million men, there were very few true believers in the ranks. This was an army of draftees, precious few of whom had ever fully believed in "the cause". Neither this book, nor the volume that follows, are political books, but as we read, it becomes harder to separate the experience of the soldiers from the political decisions that sent them over there to fight.

The portrait emerging from these readings is of young Americans (some barely out of their teens) with little knowledge of the history, and precisely none of the countries they found themselves in, thrust into a totally hostile environment, facing an enemy that was indistinguishable from the civilian population they had been sent to protect, an enemy fighting on its home ground, and having at least twenty years experience of guerrilla warfare.

Geography and climate, too, in the form of the jungle, proved to be an implacable impediment to victory (almost a harbinger of defeat). A leitmotiv in the narrative spells it out: that the jungle is the enemy. Spending days and nights entangled in dense foliage, with the added fear of snakes and other venomous jungle inhabitants, the men felt trapped in a greenhouse. Their claustrophobia increased as a result of the impenetrable vegetation that blocked out the sky. On top of this was the constant fear of the enemy present, perhaps, only in the form of a booby trap, appearing and disappearing like a wraith, with a natural ability to melt back into his natural habitat.

Such were the circumstances that drove men mad—not mad in the sense of certifiably insane—but mad enough to lose their moral compass, their basic humanity, and respect for human life. The would-be liberators turned into murderers, striking out at any Vietnamese who came into view, for anyone might be a Vietcong sympathizer. This, of course, is the story of the disaster of My Lai, which took place in March 1968, six years before the end of the war. My Lai was by no means unique, although the scale of the atrocity went way beyond any similar case. It is revisited in *No Lessons Learned*.

No Lessons Learned grows out of the final chapter of *Martial Valor*. In it, Bonadeo re-visits the themes already discussed in the earlier book but here expanded, along with a broader range of sources. Since Vietnam, the United States, after a short hiatus, has been continuously involved in a series of lesser conflicts. The Iranian Islamic revolution and the fall of the Shah led to the hostage crisis, which never resulted in actual hostilities, but the consequent resentment on both sides still smolders. There was President Reagan's bombing of Tripoli, which probably provoked the terrorist attack on the Pan Am plane over Lockerbie, Scotland. There was also Reagan's proxy war against the Nicaraguan Sandinistas (the Iran-contra scandal, as it came to be known) that tainted the last years of his presidency. There was the invasion of Panama under the first President Bush. And finally, under his son, following the destruction of the New York Trade Center and the assault on the Pentagon in September 2001, America embarked on two full-scale wars in Afghanistan and Iraq. These wars have claimed the lives of more than 5000 American soldiers, and many more thousands injured, including a large number who will require psychiatric help, many for the remainder of their lives. Naturally, there are no accurate figures for the numbers of foreign civilians killed in the course of these wars, but we do know of the millions displaced from their homes and forced to leave their country.

Just to catalogue the above wars and conflicts is to underline, with Alfredo Bonadeo, the lessons not learned, both from Vietnam and from the history of warfare since World War II. The primary lesson is that foreign policy conducted in the form of military intervention abroad is almost inevitably doomed to fail. A native population, even one groaning under the oppression of a dictatorial regime, will always regard its would-be liberators as invaders. Their stated intention (to free that population from the yoke of oppression) will always arouse suspicion. Is the stated aim of an expeditionary force really liberation? Or is it the aim to capture a strategic or economic advantage?

A second lesson to be learned is that, in a very physical and cultural sense, a foreign army does not belong on alien territory. This is reflected in the literature on Vietnam (and from other wars, too) that records the profound disconnect between the soldiers sent to fight and the native population deemed to require liberation. There is a natural distance between foreign military and local citizens which can only widen into antagonism as a war progresses. What is in the initial stages might have been passive acceptance swiftly develops into active hostility, and a marked preference for any guerrilla or insurgency force (and there will be an insurgency) that may arise. The jungle in Vietnam, the desert in Iraq, and the daunting mountain ranges and ravines in Afghanistan are as hostile as the indigenous population, and ultimately impossible to conquer. Such inimical geographical facts are an eloquent statement of implacable opposition. The foreigner may come as an explorer, as a visitor, but not as a conqueror.

A further lesson to be learned from Vietnam, and every conflict since, is that war changes a man's nature, and not for the better. Lengthy exposure to a war inevitably exposes the mark of the beast, that is, the peeling away of every layer of civilizing mantle and moral restraint that over the centuries have developed a respect for one's own moral core and the lives of others. Once these have been removed, as Bonadeo rightly suggests, an individual is forever marked and permanently degraded. There are consequences to the political decision to deploy a volunteer army, which inevitably calls on a smaller pool of soldiers to carry the burden. This leads to continuous recall to combat via multiple re-deployments. The psychological consequences are predictable: post-traumatic stress disorder (PTSD) and its innumerable symptoms: anxiety, fear of death, depression, and suicidal thoughts. The pressure causes men to lose their moral compass, to the point of conceiving murderous rages against the local inhabitants, any one of whom might be an enemy or enemy sympathizer. It is this that produces a My Lai, or an Abu Ghraib, or a Habitha, where we are told that a particular squad went on a killing spree. We can add the prison camp at Guantanamo to the list, deliberately placed beyond American soil and thus beyond the reach of established American jurisprudence. This abandonment of the normal forms of law, including the right of habeas corpus is also a form of madness from which there appears to be no way out.

A final lesson not learned from Vietnam, and every conflict since is that war comes home. When it is finally over, it is not over, neither for the survivors nor those close to them. The bodies of those who fall in battle are retrieved, and returned to their families, to receive a moving burial and loving tributes from relatives and friends. But that is not the end for the family. The gap in their ranks will last the rest of their lives, and it is made worse in the case of the loss of a husband, leaving a wife and children.

Other soldiers return with loss of limbs and will have to spend the rest of their lives in rehabilitation, accustoming themselves to prostheses, to different forms of mobility, facing the prospect of a lifetime of adjustment, and the difficulty of finding a satisfying career. And then there are the hidden wounds, referred to above, the damaged psyche and its consequences, that add to the difficulties of adjustment to civilian life. These can result in broken marriages, addiction to drugs and alcohol in a vain attempt to dull the pain, frequent homelessness, explosive outbreaks of violence, and suicide. Many homeless veterans from the Afghanistan and Iraq wars have joined the company with their comrades from the Vietnam wars on the streets of American cities. Such tragic consequences should cause a society to question the rationale of continuous warfare.

The great value of the war studies undertaken by Alfredo Bonadeo is that they trigger parallels to the conflicts the country is currently engaged in. They emphasize how easy it is to get engaged in a war, and how difficult it is to get out of it. They lay out the repeated themes of what it means to take part in a war and the impact on the individual soldier, as well as the cost to society at large. They raise the question of whether it is ever possible to learn from history. As we survey the contemporary political scene, a new administration appears hell-bent on stirring up conflict with increased nationalism and a military show of power. The sad conclusion to be reached is that the lessons to be learned from these studies are undertaken with the greatest reluctance.

Harry Lawton, University of California, Santa Barbara
April, 2016

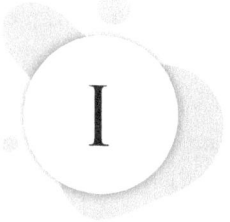

DUE CAUSE

A WAR WITHOUT A CAUSE

The cause and the combatants' belief in it have been, and still are, the central issues of almost any war. The first theorist of modern war, Karl von Clausewitz, conceded that soldiers might draw their martial spirit from enthusiasm for a cause, but he was skeptical about the benefits and viewed it as irrelevant to the performance on the battlefield. He surmised that its absence could even be an advantage to the combatant. Freedom from those political and ethical prejudices that go along with the belief in a cause would enable the soldier to become absorbed in his appointed task which is to fight with courage and abandon.[4] To instill courage, soldiers should be trained in such a way as to turn themselves into an all-powerful, primitive breed, untouched by civilization and prompted by savagery. War itself, he believed, is the main tool for bringing men back to a primitive state, one capable of turning them into hardy and bold soldiers: "Today practically no means other than war will educate a people in this spirit of boldness."[5]

Like Clausewitz, Stephen Crane did not consider the cause an essential ingredient for igniting the martial spirit in a soldier. In his novel, *The*

Red Badge of Courage, the protagonist, Henry Fleming, a soldier in the American Civil War, was heedless of the Union cause—keeping the states united and freeing the slaves. He had no notion of a higher purpose. Idle and fatuous feelings propelled him to the battlefield.[6] Dreaming of the bloody battles and heroic exploits of the ancients, his resolve to fight took shape in the peaceful tedium of his life on the farm where he imagined himself displaying exceptional prowess and daring do in front of insurmountable odds. On the night that he heard the village church bell announcing a great battle to come, he went into "a prolonged ecstasy of excitement," thinking of the war and glory it would promise. He decided to enlist. [7]

In his first defining battle Henry turned his back on the fight and ran "like a rabbit" in panic. Later, ashamed of his weakness, he projected a wild hatred for the opposing army and resolved to face it again. Pinioned by this new emotion, he was able to transform himself into "another thing," a savage in the mold of Clausewitz's soldiers. When his unit launched a crucial counterattack, he was back on the field, possessed by a rage that turned quickly into a "dark and stormy specter," leading him to "dream of abominable cruelties." He "plunged like a mad horse," struggled valiantly with the enemy, and succeeded in snatching the flag. Having tapped into his primitive, barbarous self, it became the propelling force that made him a hero in his own eyes and those of his comrades.[8] Crane showed great insight into what constitutes bravery in battle. However, as we will see in the following chapters, both Clausewitz and Crane were mistaken in discounting the value of a worthy cause in strengthening the mind and conduct of the combatant. Clausewitz relied solely on a soldier's physical attributes for building up his martial spirit. He maintained that action on the battlefield itself forges a soldier's toughness and endurance, ignoring the fact that physical qualities have limitations, while moral qualities do not. [9] Crane went deep into the psyche of his character. Henry Fleming came out of the war essentially as self-promoting and egoistic as the day he enlisted. The knowledge that he had survived while others had not, filled him with pride and underscored his moral failings toward his comrades.

Tolstoy was the first to reveal the importance of a cause as an incentive for combat. Not only was he a thinker and writer, but a soldier as well with extensive experience in the Caucasus and at Sevastopol during the Crimean War. In *War and Peace*, the Russian opposition to the French is worked out as an exploit by a people spurred by their instinctive rebellion against an enemy bent on conquest and oppression. The Russians had a cause, the defense of their land and way of life. It generated their impulse to fight. This commitment sparked a force, which Tolstoy called pure "spirit." It supported the Russians at the battle of Borodino and in their pursuit of the retreating French across the frozen steppe, spelling the end of Napoleon's Grand army.[10] Because he saw this military spirit in action, he ignored the slaughter at Borodino and called the battle a victory.[11] Moved by a worthy and powerful cause—defense against domination and oppression—an army will disregard danger and death.

S. L. A. Marshall, the foremost student of soldiers in battle in World War I and II, has concluded that the cause is decisive in the outcome of war: "Belief in a cause is the foundation of the aggressive will in battle." Moreover, if a cause is given, but an army has no "faith" in it, that army will be at the mercy of the enemy and will lose the war.[12] His view, based on observation and experience on the battlefield is shared by the novelist and Vietnam veteran, Tim O'Brien, who has written widely about the cause as a motivating force. He believes that war, any war, requires not simply a cause, but some sort of a just cause, like that of WW II, stopping Hitler and Japanese militarism. Such a cause had the power to firmly grip every combatant because its justice was recognized and individually internalized. "The justice and imperative of the cause" are essential for fighting a war.[13]

General Westmoreland, the American commander in Vietnam, declared that "we were in Vietnam for serious and moral purposes."[14] What these purposes exactly were, the general never said, and it remains doubtful whether he really believed in their value and whether or not he knew the soldiers believed in them. However, his statement showed that he, too, was aware of the role that a cause should play (or ought to have played) in the war that he and his soldiers were fighting.

Among American soldiers in Vietnam, the cause was conspicuous for its absence. This held true as well for the South Vietnamese. Some people have claimed that heavy losses by the South Vietnamese (11,000 dead and 21,600 wounded in 1965) were evidence that they were fighting for a cause, but this ignored the fact that those casualties were suffered "passively," that is, by units entrenched in forts or ambushed on roads rather than engaged in offensive operations.[15] The South Vietnamese were not collectively committed and consequently reluctant to shed their blood trying to kill their own people. The North Vietnamese under the umbrella of the National Liberation Front were fighting to unite the country after years of colonial abuse and to achieve independence from foreign domination. It was essentially a civil war between the faction that supported the puppet regime of Ngo Dinh Diem and the followers of Ho Chi Minh. It was full of ambiguities, one veteran recalled, legal, moral, and historical that made it impossible for a cause to take shape in the minds of Americans who became uncertain and confused. "You don't kill people, and you don't die when everything is so ambiguous." For a cause to be worthy, it must be deeply felt by the individual combatant. As for himself, this veteran confessed that his pride moved him to enlist—"nothing positive, no dreams of glory or honor, just to avoid the blush of dishonor."[16] This may have been sufficient reason to enlist, but he would face death with a great deal of fear and would kill with much regret.

Such was the experience of many combatants, and the result was not a hymn of triumph, but a dirge of anguish. Many protagonists of the war acknowledged the absence of a cause. A doctor in the field was moved to define the war as "strange," as he came to realize that the soldiers were fighting "for something they didn't believe in or for that matter, didn't care about." They only cared about serving for 365 days, the prescribed length of each soldier's tour, and then leaving Vietnam.[17] Without a commitment that would give strength and meaning to their deeds, the soldiers killed to save themselves or simply to show a good body count which was General Westmoreland's directive aimed at documenting American success. Under such circumstances, the combatants' enthusiasm for fighting eventually faded. They simply went through the motion of serving and fighting. "Patrols, sweeps, missions, search and destroy," noted an observant doctor assigned to the Marine camp at Phu Bai, "continued every day as if part of sunlight itself." Even the colonel in charge of that unit unconsciously revealed at daily briefings the purposelessness of it all: "It seemed that one important purpose of patrols was for them merely to take place, to happen, to exist; there had to be patrols. It gave the men something to do. Find the enemy, make contact, kill, be killed, and return." [18] The colonel tried to inject some sense into these futile endeavors by explaining how effectively the Americans were keeping the enemy off balance. However, he was unable to point to any sign of progress. The soldiers' energy and sacrifice had been expended into a vacuum, giving them every reason to be distressed.

Besides inducing a mindless repetition of useless actions, the lack of a cause had the power to render death a traumatic experience for the survivors. They felt the loss of friends and comrades on the battlefield to be a waste. The knowledge that they had died for no "higher purpose" was "a hard pill to swallow." In his memoir, *A Rumor of War*, Lieutenant Philip Caputo brooded about the fallen and felt "an emptiness, a sense of futility." This melancholic pondering coupled with his closeness to the dead whose records, as "The Officer in Charge of the Dead," he kept for a while, led him to the brink of suicide.[19]

At the center of the narrative *in Going After Cacciato*, the soldiers were more than discouraged. Spiritlessly they soldiered on, not knowing if it was a war of ideology or economics or hegemony or spite. They did not know how to feel when they saw villages burning. Revenge? Loss? Peace of mind or anguish?" Without a higher purpose they had become disoriented, and in the end lost their sense of good and evil.[20] They acted like automatons; they killed and died simply because "they were embarrassed not to," because of personal pride, or because of youthful arrogance. One veteran, knowing that he had gone to war without a cause he could believe in, called himself a coward for joining up.[21] Ironically, refusing to enlist in such a circumstance could be called courageous; joining the fight, is a sign of cowardice.

In *Going After Cacciato*, the American unit came across Captain Rhallon of the Iranian secret service. He belonged to a foreign culture, yet he knew about the problem with American soldiers. He knew they were failing because they were fighting without a cause. "Purpose," he lectured them, provides the combatant with "moral imperatives" and enables him to fight hard, well, and winningly. "Without a purpose, men will run," Captain Rhallon concluded, as the fleeing Cacciato and his wandering unit have shown. But the purpose must be right and good. You, soldiers, are fighting to suppress the independence of the Vietnamese people. This, he said, is not a worthy cause. It has the effect of jeopardizing the individual ego and demeaning his self-respect. They were failing, not because they lacked military supplies, but because they lacked the spirit that a deeply felt cause would engender. "It is purpose that keeps men at their post—only purpose," the Captain insisted.[22]

No one would say that the Germans and the Japanese in World War II were not infused with a military spirit. They fought hard and bravely and claimed many victories. But because world domination was an outworn cause—a regression, one might add to the political thinking of an earlier time when to conquer and dominate was the respected norm, they could find no support outside their circle of influence. When the world came to recognize their purpose, and they ran out of supplies, no nation would help them. They were bound for defeat, for they had neither morality nor justice on their side. Sadly, the ideals embodied in the cause that animated the generation that fought in Europe and the Pacific were betrayed in Vietnam. Whereas justice was present in the hearts and minds of America and her Allies during World War II, this was not a fundamental basis for U.S. military action in Vietnam. The purpose promoted by the government failed to inspire American soldiers who were psychologically unprepared to make the ultimate sacrifice. "What really bothered me," one veteran said, "were some of the things I saw that were not compatible with the standards that I had been brought up to believe in terms of being a member of the military and fighting for a country that heroically helped defeat the Germans and the Japanese."[23]

Those standards were betrayed by the violent and savage way in which the war was conducted, primarily, the carelessness and lack of control among the higher ranks that resulted in the indiscriminate killing of Vietnamese citizens. Many who had enlisted to serve the mythical motherland that America represented, soon abandoned the idea when they came to the battlefield and saw its brutalities: "Blowing up villages and tearing up rice fields with tanks and amphibious tractors," bullying old men and women and generally running around with your rifle and your name shooting anything that moved"[24] made it impossible for the combatants to embrace a cause. Random shooting and killing denied the basis for the democracy that Washington promoted as the proper defense against Communism. No one on the battlefield could honestly claim that these massacres served a just cause. The uncertainty and ambiguity that the ensuing void generated pained the combatants. A veteran and a poet in despair asked: "And when we next go out again/ At night to kill more killer men/ Or else be hunted to our end/ Will it prove the Cause is ours?"[25]

Killing proved nothing; it had become an end in itself. A veteran and novelist with extensive combat experience offered this reason for fighting: Americans and Vietnamese fight and destroy one another because they "are here. It is like two scorpions in a jar. They'll kill each other, but only because they're in the jar." [26] While this kind of mechanical response to the enemy could rightly be ascribed to American soldiers, it had little in common with their enemies, the Viet Cong. The Viet Cong possessed what the Americans lacked, "a moral certainty so strong as to make the suffering of individuals invisible," a certainty resting on the belief that they were defending their country's independence and that their fight was just. The spirit animating the North explains how it was possible for a people of tiny men, no bigger than boys, to succeed in driving out of their country a "race of giants." They "had seemed so motivated, as if history were riding on their shoulders," said a former Marine lieutenant who returned to Vietnam fifteen years later in a personal quest for the meaning of the war. He came to understand that the North Vietnamese "saw death not as a tragedy but as part of a higher purpose. Like the Texans who fought to the death at the Alamo, they were ready to sacrifice themselves." Contrarily, the Americans neither had a comparable goal nor the moral certainty of a cause that would enable them to summon the spirit necessary to fight winningly. They killed because they had to. Many soon realized that the country that had sent them to fight and die "didn't believe in what [it was] doing," and it wasn't long before the Viet Cong sensed their lack of will. [27] A North Vietnamese professor who was imprisoned in South Vietnam, asked the journalist, Bernard Fall, "Do the Americans think they can stay with this kind of war for 30, 40 years? Because that is what this is going to take."[28] The opponents of the Diem regime were fighting oppression, both political and economic. They stood their ground and stayed the course. Fall correctly foresaw that unless the Diem regime undertook "true" economic and political reforms, even "the hugest military power in the world can be stalemated" for a long time by lightly armed peasant guerrillas and the infantry of a tiny underdeveloped country. [29]

Why did the Americans lack a cause that would have inspired the military spirit? Of course, a cause did exist; namely, to stop communist expansion in Southeast Asia and to sustain an advantage over the Soviet Union. President Johnson speaking in April 1965 rhetorically asked: "Why are we in Vietnam? Because we have a promise to keep to the people of South Vietnam... and to strengthen world order."[30] The rationale was too abstract and ideologically motivated, not something the soldiers and the public would embrace emotionally. It was not "a credible, widely accepted justification for American involvement."[31] This failure to spark the fighting spirit was shown, for instance, by the lame reason given by the officers of a battalion promotion board who tried to impress on a private that the incentive for fighting was simply to win. There was no attempt to explain what winning would mean to Vietnam and America.[32] The result was that the American soldier acted under the force of habit, self-preservation, and revenge, rather than under a forward-moving impulse. As previously stated, General Westmoreland had declared early on that Americans were fighting for serious moral purposes, but he avoided defining these purposes and failed to exhort his soldiers to embrace them. His press conferences never revealed that he believed in any cause. He never mentioned any, and consequently failed to motivate his soldiers. He neither predicted when the war would end, nor forecast the beginning of the end or when a corner would be turned, or if there was a corner. He would only say that there was progress and that the more men he had, the more progress he would make. [33] Yet the Military Command knew that the war aims ought to have been clearly defined, that it ought to have set forth a cause for the soldiers and public to believe in. How large the failure was in providing the basic guidelines can be gathered from the rules in force at the time. The rules called for a definition of the war's purpose: "Not until the political purpose has been determined and defined by the President and the Congress," Colonel Summers pointed out in his assessment, "can strategic and tactical objectives be clearly identified." Seventy per cent of the Army generals who managed the war were uncertain of its objectives, and their ambiguities were felt on the battlefield by soldiers with little motivation.[34]

While America's previous wars were fought in the heat of passion, this war was fought in "cold blood."[35] What is meant by "passion" is unclear, but generally passion comes from an emotion generated by a deeply felt belief. From this, it can be rightly assumed that it is the quality of a cause that creates the passion that nails the energy and resolve of the combatants. The American people had the instinctive knowledge that this war was being fought for ends that were less than noble and far from vital to their interests. Their lack of passion for it underlay the combatants' lack of resolve. As a whole, the country did not accept opposition to Communism in Southeast Asia as a valid cause for war. The "hawks" who believed it was valid, upheld a mythical land of brave, freedom-loving South Vietnamese, one which had been celebrated by various presidents—Eisenhower, Kennedy, and Johnson—but which in fact had never existed.[36]

Cause or no cause, what played a central role in United States' belligerency in Vietnam was the knowledge of and pride in its exceptional power. A powerful nation must maintain its reputation, and the political establishment believed that America had global responsibilities. Ominously, the discharge of those responsibilities seemed to be the function, not of wisdom or altruism, but of her military power alone.[37] Vietnam was an opportunity to display that power. The mere possession of great national power, such as America enjoyed after 1945, made it difficult for its leaders to resist projecting it far and wide.[38] It ought to be clearly displayed to avert any and all enemies. To advertise American exceptionalism— this was the motivating factor and the unadmitted cause for fighting. Washington thought that, once confronted by American power, the North Vietnamese would realize that they could never win. They would reduce hostilities, and eventually give up.[39] As Dean Rusk explained, when a great nation like the United States of America pursues its goals, it engages itself in such a way as to cause the enemy to yield. It was an argument based on the belief that when pitted against American troops, the Vietnamese would cave, that American troops with their firepower, air support, helicopters, and tanks would simply be too much for them.[40] As a consequence, Americans discarded half measures and compromise. The power of arms would be the proper means to deal with the enemy. Nixon criticized President Johnson's gradual escalation of the air and ground war because he believed it was an insufficient way for the U.S. to show its power and prevail. Gradual escalation, he thought, would convince the enemy that the United States lacked the will to win. One unidentified South Vietnamese official urged Nixon to use the "great economic and military power" of the U.S. and force the enemy to settle. He and the rest of the South Vietnamese leaders, the official explained, understood the nature of the Viet Cong very well and could confidently say that they would stop at nothing short of winning everything. He warned, "We cannot compromise with them, and we cannot negotiate with them. This has to be a fight to the finish." Nixon heard from the same official what no doubt he wanted to hear, "With your help and support, we are ready to fight them and beat them." [41]

Reliance on power was real enough after all. Americans went to war in Vietnam never doubting a victorious finish. They believed their superior weaponry and technology would enable them to prevail. [42] Whatever the objective of the war—and many in Washington failed to define the objective with any precision—American leaders were certain that their superior technology would carry them. In 1966, Henry Cabot Lodge, U.S. Ambassador to South Vietnam (1963—64) complacently declared, "I think that among the Vietnamese there is a feeling that once the Viet Cong and Hanoi have been convinced that their attempt at aggression is doomed to fail, they will stop." [43] Faith in American exceptionalism fed faith in its "invincibility" so that Washington continued to support the war even when it became unacceptable to the American public and victory appeared out of reach.[44] Opposition to communism supplied American leadership with sufficient reason to rattle her weapons. Communism was a strongly evocative system that stood for everything capitalism opposed, and unless it was stopped, so Washington claimed, it would spread throughout the countries of Southeast Asia. Therefore, saving South Vietnam from communism was the right thing to do.[45] Fifteen years after Dean Rusk announced in 1949 that the resources of the United States would be deployed "to reserve Indochina and Southeast Asia from further Communist encroachment," Washington believed the alleged threat was enough to mobilize the energy and minds of soldiers and citizens for all-out war.[46] Lyndon Johnson's fear of being branded "soft on Communism" and losing the elections of 1964, was reason enough for him to support it. If the United States were unable to stop Communism, he declared, they "must surrender the Pacific" and then defend their own shores![47] This very aggressive, fear-inducing ideology became the principal cause for going to war. Curbing Communism may have appeared to be a sufficient reason, but the threat was not close enough to home to inspire the aggression necessary to succeed. After all, Ho Chi Minh was not out to conquer the world. His agenda lay purely within Vietnamese borders. Neither had the U.S. been physically attacked. Moreover, the nature of the proposed military involvement (a guerrilla war with no identifiable enemy and no taking of territory) was at odds with the understanding of the nature of war that had been incorporated into American experience since at least the beginning of the twentieth century. Fear of Communism was not prevalent or powerful enough to rouse the public into supporting an invasion. This fact greatly disturbed General Westmoreland who decrying the American "yearning for peace and disarmament," implicitly incited the country to shift their yearnings instead, toward armament, belligerence, and fighting.[48]

But anti-communism never became a galvanizing cause. It failed because the majority of soldiers and civilians eventually perceived it as nothing more than an official pretext. A well-known combatant who gave everything he had in a fight to the death, declared anti-communism counterproductive, "We weren't stopping communism here. We were stomping communism into Vietnam, and it kept sprouting again with a thousand branches."[49]

Anti-communism was an excuse. The real cause was the American triumph of power. Washington's reluctance to negotiate was evidence that its true aim was to show off its military might. In 1965 President Johnson declared that talk of negotiations would only further weaken South Vietnamese morale.[50] In the waning days of Johnson's presidency, General Westmoreland still believed that military power was the infallible instrument of American policy and success. He told the president that he should keep in mind that American power in Vietnam was at its height and that if he agreed to negotiate, the talk should aim at reinforcing the United States' reputation for power. This alone should decide the negotiations 'outcome, he urged, because, from it, the enemy would be forced to accept American terms.[51] The only force would get the Communists to desist from fighting. At that time, Johnson had serious reservations about a British-Soviet peace initiative, fearing that it would make Washington appear desperate for negotiations. He berated Senator Church for advocating a negotiated American withdrawal and opted for a complete "disavowal" of negotiations.[52] Even though his position was far from dovish, it still failed to satisfy the hawks. Nixon surmised that Johnson's talk and behavior suggested that "we only want peace, that we want to negotiate" which would prolong the war rather than win it.[53] For Westmoreland, too, negotiations would lengthen the war; they showed weakness and meant nothing but "surrender by degree."[54] The end result of negotiating would mean renouncing the use of force, and America wanted to display her prime and matchless asset. But going to the brink and over the edge failed as a just cause for fighting; it was unconvincing to both the combatants and the country. It left the minds and hearts of soldiers on the battlefield cold.

Still, there were a few whose belief in it bred a fanatic resolve to fight. These were the Green Berets. An example of their undaunted military spirit was described by Robin Moore in his account of an action defending an American camp, "Another American sergeant wearing his green beret jumped over the wall, rallying the strikers behind him," and "the impact of the fighting was irresistible; shouting like a combatant, I leaped out of the safety of the bunker and ran for the wall. Looking down at the savage fight below, I could scarcely control the near-unconquerable impulse to jump. On the walls wounded strikers still able to fire weapons kept up a blast at the new squads unendingly breaching the outer perimeter." These special forces were trained to risk their lives in a distant country. Scharne, the central character in Moore's book, *The Green Berets*, explains: "I am a professional soldier and I take orders and do what I am told. Second, I don't want my children fighting the Communists at home." He vows that he and his comrades will fight forever in those undeveloped nations that "are targets of Communist expansion."[55] Such enthusiasm might lead one to believe they were professional warriors eager for any opportunity to unleash their primitive instincts and show their skill. Yet, it is clear they had accepted unquestioningly the official cause ignored by others, namely, stopping the expansion of Communism. It stirred the emotion that sparked their bravery. But the skepticism and indifference of the majority of combatants and non-combatants alike indicated that the apparent purpose was not worthy of the sacrifices Americans were asked to make in Vietnam.

Nevertheless, duty and patriotism prevailed in many soldiers who, though indifferent to the anti-communist cause, fought very hard. The combatants of *We Were Soldiers Once... and Young*, a memoir of the fighting that engaged a battalion of the 1st Cavalry in the battle of Ia Drang, fought with no doubt, no indecision, and no inner torment. They went to war because their country asked them to go and because the President ordered it. "We went where we were sent because we loved our country. We went to war because our country asked us to go," and because "we saw it as our duty to go." This was enough to supply them with the necessary resolve and energy to fight. On being wounded one of them is hit by "fear, real fear." But it is not paralyzing, "Fear comes, but once you recognize it and accept it, it passes just as fast as it comes, and you don't think about it anymore." Fear cannot stop any of them, and the veterans will remember that the battle had "many heroes, but no cowards." Everyone lost friends, but what counted was that "the bravery they showed on the battlefield will live forever." Another soldier recalled that for two hours he was alone with his gun, shooting at the enemy. "Enemies were shooting at me and bullets were hitting the ground beside me and cracking above my head. I fired as fast as I could in long bursts. My M-60 was cooking." Specialist Clarence Jackson took a round clean through his left hand, shifted his rifle to his right, and continued firing until he was hit a second time. "Sergeant Vasquez and several of the other wounded men likewise fought on, thanks to their own courage... Sergeant Ruben Thompson was struck by a bullet above his heart that exited under his left arm; bleeding heavily he grabbed a rifle and fought on." Specialist Parish "delivered lethal fire on wave after wave of the enemy until he ran out of ammunition." Then standing up under fire with a .45 pistol in each hand, he "fired clip after clip into the enemy, who were twenty yards out; he stopped their attack." Another company holds its ground against the North Vietnamese and does it "in a stunning display of personal courage and unit discipline. They held their positions and died fighting."[56] The fearless soldiers that enliven the pages of *We Were Soldiers Once –and Young* were honoring their commitment to serve in the United States Armed Forces. Animated purely by soldierly pride and skill, they did not question the legitimacy of the war.

Other soldiers fought solely for the pure love of fighting. For Lieutenant Hodges "it was the fight that mattered, not the cause. It was the endurance that was important, the will to face certain loss, unknown dangers, unpredictable fates." He felt like this because he belonged to a family with a proud military tradition that gave him "an inherited right to violence. His pride accumulated with every engagement, even as the reason for it grew more amorphous."[57] For some who also disdained the official cause, the need to submit to the circumstances in the field, to take risks, suffer, and die was the sole rationale for fighting. The purpose resided simply in accomplishing the assigned mission. Once assigned a "mission," Lieutenant Martin of *Going after Cacciato* argued, one is bound to the tactics and strategy devised by the leadership and to pay the price if there is one to pay. He claimed that "neither purpose nor cause" is the most important element. Battles are fought "among human beings, not purposes," and fighting was a test of one's personal qualities. It was a soldier's duty toward himself to use all his resources. Lieutenant Martin hoped that his men would understand why he required them to unnecessarily risk their lives searching enemy tunnels before blowing them up, and why they should march up mountains without a single rest. The purpose was not to prevail over the enemy, but to exercise their full capacities of courage, endurance, and will- power, in short, to prove their manliness. Thus, he did have a purpose and a cause, and to implement it, he ordered needless maneuvers and abusive treatment. He notified them that anyone who during a march might fall by the wayside because of exhaustion or sunstroke would be left where he falls.[58] This kind of abuse, whatever the cause, was likely to alienate them from the war effort, and persuade them to neglect, rather than respect their duty.

Despite the spread of anti-communist propaganda, the majority of Americans were not taken up by the war effort. As the military ran out of volunteers and the draft was instituted, protests erupted on college campuses. By 1968, people had taken to the streets in every corner of the nation. Naturally, the resistance at home was felt by the combatants. Too late, Secretary McNamara discovered the vital value of the country's support; it was more important than all other material of war. "A nation's deepest strength," he wrote in his memoir, lies not in its military prowess but, rather, in the unity of its people. "We overestimated the effect of South Vietnam's loss on the security of the West." The South Vietnamese were not highly motivated, and "we built a progressively more massive effort on an inherently unstable foundation."[59] He came to understand that such unified support, essential to the success of a military enterprise, was non-existent in the United States. The public protests infected the soldiers, rendering them unresponsive to the mission that the politicians and generals had assigned them.

That hostility was critical in changing the opinion and conduct of Lieutenant Lewis Puller, a Marine whose father was a famous general. When he enlisted, he embraced anti-communism and military duty equally, but on returning home, he saw how the veterans were "shunned and reviled" just when they needed some form of validation for their sacrifices, just when they needed support in a troublesome period of adjustment to civilian life. The people's indifference toward the returning veterans forced on him the realization that he had made the wrong choice in volunteering. His regret at having "given myself to a cause that allowed me no pride for having been a participant," [60] would confirm Secretary McNamara's belated admission that the value of the country's support was more important than all other material of war.

The majority of combatants belonged to the lower strata of society. Although 79% of army troops had at least a high school education, many recruits were still teenagers with little intellectual or life experience that would enable them to understand and embrace a cause. Most were too young to vote or drink legally. They went to war because they were drafted. Instead of upping the draft age, Congress lowered the voting and drinking age. In Lieutenant Broyles's unit, for instance, most of them were high school dropouts. They served with little understanding of the reason for fighting. Unfortunately, these kids and others from disadvantaged backgrounds were twice as likely than their better-off peers to serve in the military and see combat. Broyles knew many who had studied at Rice and Oxford, and none of them went to Vietnam. In the Harvard class of 1970, of the twelve hundred classmates only fifty-six entered the military and just two went to Vietnam. The upper crust who volunteered were regarded by their peers as "suckers having to risk their lives in a wrong war, in a wrong place, at the wrong time."[61] Because men from disadvantaged backgrounds could not avail themselves of the connections and exemptions that would allow them to avoid service, their attitude was mainly to rid themselves of an obligation as quickly as possible: "The time thing of 365 days just nailed it down," the doctor in the field noted, "365 days and not a second more." Behind them, there were only the shouts and murmurs of disgruntled people. The end of their tour was their coveted goal. To these men "Nam simply didn't count for anything in itself. It was something they did between this and that, and they did what they had to do to get through it—no more." [62] General Westmoreland himself confirmed that the sons of working-class Americans did most of the soldiering in Vietnam. The only Americans who bore the burden, made a sacrifice and paid the price, he wrote in his memoir, were those on the battlefield, and those were "mainly the poor man's sons." [63] The combatants well knew it. With few exceptions, one of them recorded, that the sons of working-class Americans "did the soldiering and the dying in Vietnam." [64] The poor and uneducated, black and white, comprised the mass of the infantry with the result that they took a disproportionately high percentage of casualties. [65] Among them, there was no overriding "cause." The members of the wealthier and better educated knew how to manipulate the system to avoid military duty. For many, it was a matter of principle, and to avoid the draft, they escaped to Canada. Of those who, believing in the official rationale, enlisted voluntarily, many found their belief misplaced when the unexpected effects of the violence on their bodies and souls, crippled them physically and mentally. In the struggle, their faith turned out to be less than enduring, and the cause evaporated.

One example of this was the experience of Ron Kovic. As a teenager, he "wanted to be a hero." The recruiters from the Marine corps who spoke to the senior class at his high school made a profound impression on him. He felt as if his dream was being realized right there and then. The recruiters told him that the Marine Corps built men by strengthening body, mind, and spirit, just the kind of strength that would enable an ordinary man to become a hero. In his youthful naiveté, Kovic had an uncritical and shallow idea of heroism. The celluloid heroes, Audie Murphy of To Hell and Back and John Wayne in The Sands of Iwo Jima, kept his dream alive. He found Murphy "so brave" that when he saw him in action chills went up and down young Kovic's spine. But the true hero was John Wayne who, while the Marine hymn played in the background, ran up a hill and was shot down just before reaching the top. [66] Kovic's cause was the quintessence of military duty—heroism. Initially, he was able to sustain the faith that ruled his youth, and he fought bravely. On the occasion that he led an assault on a village held by the Viet Cong, he wanted to prove "that I was a brave man. No matter what happened out there, I thought to myself, I could never retreat. I had to be courageous." But his heroic spirit expired when, wounded and lying helpless on the ground, he was seized by the specter of death. In one stroke the basis of his cause was struck down by a bullet that tore through his spine. Nor did it occur to him that with this sacrifice, his dream of heroism was being realized. Physical pain annihilated both dream and endeavor, "I couldn't even feel my body. I was frightened to death." He disclaimed the value of his wound, the would-be proof of his heroic endeavor, "All I could feel was the worthlessness of dying right here in this place at this moment for nothing." [67] His wound would fill the rest of his life with bitterness and pain, as equally the war and the choice he made would become the object of his fierce contempt.

Lieutenant Puller went to war to find a "meaningful direction" in his life and to search for "something larger" than himself, glory and victory for his country. Moreover, he felt an urgent and compelling need to prove himself worthy of his father, a Marine Corp general. When the lieutenant became isolated during a firefight and his gun jammed, he started running away from the enemy and toward company headquarters. As he retreated a booby-trapped howitzer round exploded and severed both his legs. The physical suffering became an equally painful inner experience. He was ashamed. In his eyes, the retreat was a cowardly act: "I spent my last healthy moments in Vietnam running from the enemy. I had failed to prove myself worthy of my father's name and was broken both in spirit and body." Like Ron Kovic, he did not see his wound as a heroic sacrifice made for a cause or the country. Rather, coupled with the lack of popular support at home, it served to release his inner doubts about the war, and he concluded that Vietnam was no field for glory. The amputation of his legs was almost a relief. It was a way out of a war that now appeared to him less than worthless. "I knew I had finished serving my time in the hell of Vietnam." [68] The wound marked a turning point in Puller's vision. The war was unworthy of his sacrifice, and he repudiated it. The attitude of the people at home made his rejection harsh and final. In the U.S. he could not vent his grief and frustration, because his talk made those around him uncomfortable. Most were embarrassed by his troubles. He personally knew many who ignored his searing experience which made him wonder how the cause could be valid when nobody wanted to discuss it with the very soldiers who had been there. He was one of the many vets who needed some form of validation because the cause he had embraced had destroyed his youth and turned him into a deformed being for the rest of his life. He came to realize that his sacrifice was worthless. Unable to discover a higher purpose for the wasted lives of his many friends who had not come home, he rejected anyone connected to the war, "I began to despise the government and the Marine Corps, which had asked of us everything and given back almost nothing." He regarded his enlistment and service as the result of an "obscene fraud" perpetrated on him by the government and the military. To ease the consequences and his sorrow he turned to alcohol and eventually committed suicide.[69]

Not only did bodily wounds lead soldiers to forsake the official cause, but the conduct of the war itself was enough to undermine it. Lieutenant Philip Caputo joined the Marine Corps because he confessed, that he was seduced by the myth engendered by John Kennedy—that there was nothing we could not do because we were Americans and that whatever we did was right. And war, like any other thing we did, would be the right thing to do. Also, something personal moved him to enlist. Like Kovic and Crane's protagonist in *The Red Badge of Courage*, it was to seize the "chance to live heroically." At home, they had enjoyed the security, comfort, and peace of an uneventful life. Just as dreams of heroism had ignited Henry Fleming's imagination and led him to yearn for "danger, challenges, and violence," so Lieutenant Caputo wanted to live the heroic experience through war, which he conceived as "the ultimate adventure." He believed that he and his comrades were to check the expansion of communism and spread American democracy around the world. They saw themselves as champions of "a cause that was destined to triumph." Their disillusionment began with the battlefield experience. The fact that they were fighting a guerrilla war on enemy territory made conventional theories of strategy and tactic obsolete. There were no set-piece battles in which the enemy could be identified and fought on equal terms. Moreover, American commanders ignored what is the basis of any well-conducted war—making territorial conquests and holding on to them. Caputo saw fighting being reduced to "a slow, steady trickle of blood" drawn in a series of ambushes and firefights. Nothing ever really changed on the battlefield. Men were killed and wounded, and patrols kept going out to fight in the same places they had fought the week before and the week before that. [70] A cause would never assert itself through the use of this strategy, and within a few months Caputo understood that he and his comrades were, in fact, fighting a war of attrition, a strategy widely used in World War I that consisted in the willful grinding down of men. It offered Americans no chance of victory and demanded many casualties. The realization completely eroded his faith in the war and its aims. At the same time, he became aware of the fact that the enemy was far more resolved and lethal than Americans had assumed. They were losing more men than expected, and many soldiers were demonstrating a skepticism that undermined their fighting spirit. For him, the cause had lost all meaning and value, and because his unit took very few prisoners and could claim no territory, his action in the field became a dismal experience. How can we, a combatant-poet ask of himself and his comrades, who are lost in the dark of "primeval night," ever "know we're right?" [71] It was a question that could be legitimately asked by Lieutenant Caputo and his men. There was no uplifting vision in that darkness, no worthwhile cause to be discerned, yet they had to face another day on the edge of death. In the end, Caputo rejected the cause that had originally led him into battle and embraced a new one—the defense of life. He gradually realized that for him and his comrades, there was "no other cause than our own survival." [72] He was one of many combatants for whom survival became the only cause. Adding fuel to this, was the soldiers' resentment for those commanders who disregarded their lives. "And who are the young men we are asking to go into action against such solid odds?" a general, alluding to the troops who were regularly sent into the field, rhetorically asked a war correspondent. The general himself supplied the reply: "They are the best we have... and they know they are at the end of the pipeline. That no one cares. They know."[73] It is inconceivable that soldiers forced to resign themselves to a futile death would believe in anything worth fighting for outside of sheer survival. Kovic too, realized that the military leaders couldn't care less whether the troops believed in a cause or not. They wanted soldiers that could be sent to the end of the pipeline, soldiers who obeyed orders, and who made sacrifices without asking questions. "He had never been anything but a thing to them [war managers]," Kovic wrote, "a thing to put a uniform on and... to run through the meat-grinder, a cheap small nothing to make mincemeat out of." [74] Officers who did care about the safety of their men were rare, and when one showed up, the grunts singled him out, as they did Lieutenant Corson in *Going After Cacciato*, a platoon leader whom the men "could finally love," because he had a great deal of respect for life: "He took no chances, he wasted no lives. The war... scared him."[75]

The war "was an evil thing done to a lot of people,"[76] and in "a barbarous, inhumane war" fought for uncertain reasons, it became "really conspicuous that there wasn't a lot of political support for [it]."[77] In the U.S. politicians talked about winning the war by increasing the forces while ignoring how the troops were being treated. On the ground, they "moved like mules," taking sniper fire by day and mortar fire by night. Endless marches in the jungle and bush consumed their bodies and souls. The brutality and uncertain military goals made it impossible for many to even think they could find a cause. The applied tactics were ineffective in securing victory. They stifled the fighting spirit and caused many combatants to question their own and their country's motives. One reason Lieutenant Caputo lost faith was his dismay at one of the standard procedures on the battlefield, the Search and Destroy operation. The soldiers were often ambushed and devastated by sudden explosions of mines or booby traps, and the enemy could not be engaged. It frustrated and embittered them. On his way to one of these operations, Caputo and his men were flying over an endless rain forest called Annamese Cordillera. It looked "hostile and utterly alien." The mission was to find one battalion, a few hundred men, in that immense area, a kind of jungle sea, where the whole North Vietnamese army might have concealed itself. "And we were going to look for a battalion," Caputo recalled in disbelief, "we were going to find a battalion and destroy it. Search and destroy." Rarely did these operations achieve the intended results. They cruelly exposed the fact that Americans were fighting a war without a front, flanks, or rear.[78] The futility could be seen in the eyes of Caputo's men—a blank expression that reflected their inner emptiness. He called it the "thousand-yard stare." The persistent failure of this strategy inspired "a hatred for everything and everyone around you." Lieutenant Caputo, himself, was weighed down by extraordinary tiredness, deeper than mere fatigue, a tiredness "that reaches down into a part of myself that I cannot name."[79] Had he been possessed of a cause greater than his individual self, it might have lifted his depression, but the opposing forces thwarted whatever sustenance could come from it. Search and Destroy operations only made the soldiers feel their powerlessness with the realization that the enemy had the upper hand. It frightened and depressed them. If they had ever believed in a cause, the use of this tactic undermined it by forever reminding them of vain efforts in a war that was impossible to win.

Search and Destroy missions put the combatant in close contact with the brutality of an environment which was universally recognized by the Americans as the real "enemy." The effort employed in resisting the effects of this enemy sapped their energy and will. They marched through jungles and rice paddies, plodding along, oppressed by the heat, "toiling up the hills and down into the paddies and across the rivers and up again and down, just humping, one step and then the next and then another." There was no mental activity, no striving for advantage. "The hump was everything, a kind of inertia, a kind of emptiness, a dullness of desire and intellect and conscience and hope and human sensibility."[80] The heat and environment could not be vanquished by force of arms, something that the

Americans had and of which they were proud. Confined in a furnace-like enclosure, they realized that the force of nature was immeasurably superior to their weaponry and willpower. It came down to "a fight against heat, thirst, poisonous insects, endless marches, jungle rot, sunburn, chapped and cracked lips and noses, and "intricate and constant patterns of pain from joints and muscles."[81] They carried on a bitter fight with this ruthless and invincible enemy. Whatever inspiration and energy a cause might have lent them, would have been defeated by the forces of a singularly hostile nature. And the other enemy, the North Vietnamese, who were ready to strike anywhere anytime, compounded their plight. The knowledge that a hidden mine or booby trap could suddenly explode engendered among them a fear that displaced all attempts at boldness. In such an environment, they could only think that the land and sun conspired with the Viet Cong, "wearing us down, driving us mad, killing us." They began to feel like victims.[82] A victim acts passively, waiting for the next blow to fall. In such a state, belief in a cause might not have helped other than to forebear the blows.

Another factor that worked against the Americans was their racial antagonism toward the Vietnamese people. This lack of sympathy was a powerful indictment of the "anti-communist crusade." One veteran writes that none of the banana groves, rice paddies, hamlets, farms, and rubber plantations "is worth the powder to blow it away with. There ain't one, not one square inch of muck within five or six thousand miles of here that I would fight anybody for, except what I'm standing on."[83] Either there was no identifying connection between the land and its people, or the connection was a hostile one, that is, the hostility of the environment mirrored an unpalatable people. This natural antagonism was abetted by the fact that the South Vietnamese fought poorly, leading many to wonder whether they cared about fighting communism and if not, whether they were worthy of defending. "Why don't the Vietnamese fight the Viet Cong like the Viet Cong fight the Vietnamese?" one helicopter pilot who had a close view of their deceptive moves on the battlefield, asked. [84] A bleak cynicism for the South permeated the ranks, as shown by this grim joke, "What you do is you load all the Friendlies onto ships and take them out to the South China Sea. Then you bomb the country flat. Then you sink the ships."[85] If the South Vietnamese were not committed, then the prime cause for fighting—opposition to the spread of communism—was even more meaningless.

The cumulative effect of the entire war scene for the ordinary soldier was simply waiting for his tour of duty to run out so that, if still alive, he could return home. Simply keeping alive gradually became the cherished cause of most Americans in Vietnam. In his memoirs, Secretary McNamara ignored both the loathing of the combatants for fighting an unwinnable war and the public protests and desire for peace. Instead, he placed a high value on the soldiers' deaths, for he believed sacrifice in and of itself an honorable offering. Death in battle, he believed, was capable of redeeming everything and anything that had gone wrong with the war. While he conceded that the American effort in Vietnam may have been "unwise," he declared that the thousands of young men sacrificed for that effort were "noble." The sacrifice endures, he proclaimed, implying that the folly of the effort was redeemed by the blood spilled. "Let us validate and honor it."[86]

The unavoidable conclusion that a misguided and unworthy cause is redeemed by the sacrifices made is dangerously wrong. An argument such as McNamara's which places a high value on personal sacrifice would justify any war, since the deaths that occurred therein, would elevate it. A more honest appraisal would be to call their deaths tragic, rather than allow the human sacrifice to ennoble questionable enterprises and deny the essential critical thinking that would lead to an analysis of what went wrong and a re-evaluation of human life vs death. Not only are such wars in danger of being repeated, but the end result of justifying war for the sake of its "heroic sacrifices" is to needlessly extend it in time. Sacrifice has always been used for the purpose of yielding a return. If such a return is not felt in an overriding and deeply felt cause by all concerned, simple victory in war is unworthy of the blood price. Excluding a religious zeal that usually includes belief in an afterlife, it would be difficult if not impossible to rouse the fighting spirit in those who place the highest value on an individual's life on earth. But McNamara's speculations took place well after the conflict ended. His argument could change neither the politics of the war nor the military strategy; neither could it comfort the disillusioned veterans.

It is hardly surprising to learn that the great majority of combatants who fought in Vietnam turned out to be "the least docile" soldiers that America has ever sent into battle. Without a cause and without the persuasion that what they were doing was good and necessary, the adversity and harassment became unbearable. Their intolerance showed up, for instance, in acts of violence against their own officers. There were other consequences. A general demoralization took hold of many who came to feel they had been "used for a purpose not worth their sweat and blood,"[87] From the end of 1969 on, the morale of the American forces deteriorated badly. The soldiers escaped into marijuana and heroin and some, stoned on these drugs that profited the Chinese traffickers and the Saigon generals, died as a result. "It was an army whose units in the field were on the edge of mutiny." Soldiers rebelled by killing officers and noncoms in "accidental" shootings and "fraggings" with grenades. As long as General Creighton Abrams kept on pursuing a war of attrition, a strategy begun with General Westmoreland, the demoralization continued.[88] By that time, fighting for a cause in Vietnam was out of the question. American soldiers would prove S.L.A. Marshall's thought, that in any conflict the belief in a cause is the root of the fighting spirit.[89] Without it, the fighting spirit was missing and the performance of a vital military duty, killing the enemy and defying death, was seriously compromised. The lack of a higher purpose deprived the soldiers of a willingness to put their lives on the line and as we will see in the following chapters, engendered among them death anxiety that undermined the performance of their duties.

II

THE KILLING

VICTIMS TO ABUSERS

It is generally assumed that military duty and patriotism motivate a soldier to fight to the death. The fact that killing on the battlefield is usually honored and rewarded supports that assumption. However, in the imagination and memory of the veterans of the Vietnam war, duty or devotion to the country was rarely the reason given for killing the enemy. Among the Americans who fought in the paddies and jungles of Vietnam, those reasons played an insignificant role. The causes that politicians and journalists spoke and wrote about also played only a minor role. Gaining the hearts and minds of the Vietnamese, defending them as the people of a republic, or forestalling the "dominoes falling" throughout Southeast Asia and ensuring the balance of power, these ideas failed to stimulate the fighting spirit of the combatants. They killed for other reasons—response to an enemy attack, desperation, vengeance, sickness—and almost always their deeds took on a personal touch. The body count directive, which placed a high value on the number of enemy corpses, provided the troops with an explicit, albeit misleading, motivation. Killing became a tool of survival in a war of attrition as the leadership and combatants came to believe that survival depended on killing as many North Vietnamese as possible. A high body count came to be regarded as a mark of success. This belief became the strongest incentive for destroying the foe.

Since killing normally depends on the decision and resolve of the perpetrator, who alone bears the responsibility for his decision and its consequences, the soldier who had no higher cause couldn't help knowing that killing reduced to simple homicide made little sense. Although it was widespread on the Vietnam battlefield, it was not necessarily, in the minds and hearts of the soldiers, a mark of real success. It is hard to find a military victory associated with killing alone. Some combatants came to regard the whole war as nothing more than institutionalized murder. A kind of slaughter divorced from war aims looked like the real cause for serving in Vietnam. "This is a slaughter," not a "defense of freedom," a reporter with the troops acknowledged.[90] A young soldier, speaking "in all bloody innocence," told another correspondent: "We are here to kill gooks. Period." [91] He had no idea about the purpose of his deeds. Many soldiers came to believe that they were indeed in Vietnam to kill gooks, not merely to support the South Vietnamese army. "That's the game out here. That's what we are here for. To kill gooks," one of them declared. This particular soldier, who was holding several wounded enemy prisoners while speaking, said that he hoped the prisoners would die so his unit could get credit for extra kills. He was silent about how they would die, but it was not improbable that he might act so as to get credit for himself. [92]

The battlefield slaughter bothered Americans at home as well. And the malaise was regarded as a problem that affected the conduct of the war. Solutions were proposed. Some students of strategy believed that the key to selling the war to the American public was to be realistic and even brutal with the public so as to harden them against the shock created by the killing, often cruel and brutal enough to inspire horror in combatants and non-combatants alike, a need that the media unfortunately ignored. "We did not kill the enemy," one strategist lamented; Instead, "we 'inflicted casualties'." Euphemisms such as this by the media only increased public skepticism. According to this strategist, brutal realism would have had the effect of getting the public used to the idea and practice of killing and making it acceptable. He thought the reporting should be stripped of its "newspeak" and aimed at justifying the unpalatable events by the demands of the politics supporting the war.[93] What these demands exactly were, was irrelevant, but the necessary approval and support of the killing were paramount, and the support of the public back home was crucial for the success of the soldiers in the field. Once reports from the battlefield were truthfully related and the aversion to warring overcome, killing and death would be turned into acceptable events. Then, the war could be waged without raising disquiet and opposition from the public.

Even though American soldiers were tormented by the necessity to do a lot of killing that made little sense, the battlefield had the power to shape their thinking and actions in unexpected ways. For them, the horrors of war were daily fare, and they could not escape the direct and indirect effects of the violence that raged. They had to adapt and transform themselves into combatants capable of defending themselves from attack. They lived and fought through the horrors of the war and were toughened by them. "I had turned mean inside," a veteran recorded the changes that happened to him as a result of his experience, "even a little cruel at times. For all my education, all my fine liberal values, I now feel a deep coldness inside me, something dark and beyond reason. It's a hard thing to admit, even to myself, but I was capable of evil."[94] Accused of murdering two Vietnamese, a lieutenant explains his outrageous act as the "result" of the war, which had awakened his lower instincts. He had been ordered to capture them, but he felt he wanted them dead instead: "Something evil had been in me that night… There was murder in my heart." His violent eruption infected the men under his command. Yet, he was unable to conceive of it as premeditated murder, "It had not been committed in a vacuum. It was a direct result of the war. The thing we had done was a result of what the war had done to us;" it had awakened "something evil in us, some dark, malicious power that allowed us to kill without feeling." At his court martial he defended his actions by arguing that he was a soldier fighting in a war whose sole aim was to kill Viet Cong and that, by implication, he had become so absorbed by the killing frenzy that he was unable to escape it. Killing with little discrimination had become an ingrained habit, and in his eyes a normal way of waging war. Of course, he knew better. As he himself admitted, he knew that "a malicious power" fed his killing zeal and allowed him and his comrades to dispatch the enemy without scruple. He knew as well that the malicious power had one source, the war and how it was conducted, "The killings had occurred in war. They had occurred, moreover, in a war... in which those ordered to do the killing often could not distinguish the Viet Cong from the civilians," a war in which the existence of "free-fire zones" gave the Americans license to do anything and everything.[95]

In besieged Khe Sanh, the Marines "got savaged a lot and softened a lot," a reporter described their state of being. Just as victims turn easily into abusers, their experience turned them into top killers. The savaging "brutalized and darkened them, and very often it made them beautiful. It took no age, seasoning, or education to make them know exactly where true violence resided. They were killers. Of course, they were. What else would anyone expect them to be?" The knowledge "absorbed them, inhabited them, made them strong in the way that victims are strong, filled them with the twin obsessions of Death and Peace." [96] They were victims of that very knowledge for it became a self-identifying trait that predisposed them to do more killing than anyone else on the battlefield. The killing was very serious business, the only business that mattered. For many Marines, it transcended military duty and became a personal affair. Revenge against an abusing enemy had nothing to do with the mission of winning a battle or war. It was an impulse created by their experience in the field. For some, it was the desire to get even with the Viet Cong who were responsible for the death of close comrades and friends. One lieutenant volunteered for a line company, even though he was close to the end of his tour and knew that he need not take the risk. But he "wanted a chance to kill somebody" to soothe his grief and hatred.[97] The experience of another soldier on his third tour sparked an impulse to kill effectively beyond control. He was the only survivor of a platoon ambushed and wiped out in the Ia Drang Valley. He survived by hiding under the bodies of his comrades while the Viet Cong went around knifing them to make sure everyone lying on the ground was dead. He barely escaped, but the experience stirred the essential emotion that made him a killer. In less than a year later, he was back on the battlefield with the Special Forces and eagerly attached himself to a unit that undertook the most daring and murderous operations. His comrades considered him a bit crazy, but also recognized that he was "a good killer, one of our best." He became a permanent member of a long-range reconnaissance patrol, a unit dedicated to ambushing the enemy, giving himself plenty of opportunities for killing. His murderous impulse became a kind of second nature that he was barely able to control. It stayed with him all the way home where he remained sitting in his room all day. He remembered putting a hunting rifle out of the window and following people and cars as they passed his house.[98]

The antagonism that fed the Americans' killing impulse had deeper roots. The successful tactics and fighting skills of the enemy, despite its manifest inferiority in arms and supplies, instilled fear and uncovered deep anxiety about death in the American soldier. The enemy came to be regarded, not as the obstacle whose elimination would ensure the freedom of South Vietnam and stop the spread of Communism in Southeast Asia, but as a threat to the health and life of the individual soldier. It was a personal matter. Eliminating the death anxiety went hand in hand with eliminating the enemy's power to destroy life. More than any other cause, official or less official, the incentive to slay the enemy had to do with silencing this anxiety.[99] Achieving relief was a personal goal more than a step toward the victory of American arms. Such was the case in a veteran novelist's long, detailed description of the steps taken to kill an enemy, his secret pride in the procedure, and his pleasure in accomplishing his goal. Killing for its own sake had become the ultimate purpose of this soldier. He was completely detached from military duty or patriotic feelings, and he destroyed the enemy without sparing any trick or effort. In the process, he was assuaging an inner torment. He reveals himself to be a cold-blooded assassin who enjoys his work:

"I raise myself straight-armed above him, bringing the bayonet roundhouse high. I gather the shirt... tightly around his neck. All I have to do is bring the knife down, drop it straight into his chest, and snap the breastbone. It would be like slicing twine. I work my fingers on the handle, feeling for a good grip. I can see nothing but his eyes, blinking from the rain... I could puncture a lung, coming straight down through the shoulders, or get his heart from the side, or simply stab him in the throat at the carotid. I let the bayonet slip from my hand and come down with all my weight on his chest, my hands around his neck. I squeeze his Adam's apple with both thumbs. I lift his head and push it back into the turf with a muted splash. My fingernails work into the back of his neck. The little man grabs both my wrists. He gurgles and works his jaw. His mouth stretches open, and he wags his tongue. Lift. Push. Squeeze. Like working a tool smoothly. His head splashes harder. His nails gouge my wrists. Lift. Push. Squeeze. Something cracks, and my thumbs work easier, deeper. His mouth and tongue make thick wet murmurs. Lift. Push. Squeeze. His body shakes as though someone is trying to yank it out from under me. His face and lips and jaw go slack. His head and hands go limp." [100]

This thorough job was the culmination of his skill as a soldier, which had as its reward an intense pleasure in every detail rather than as a necessary but distasteful step toward the successful conclusion of the war. Every detail was savored as much for the pain it inflicted on the enemy, as for the soothing of his own anxiety. He accomplished more than killing; he became as powerful as death itself (thereby mastering it).

The same personal pleasure derived from killing the enemy is found among the men from the Alpha company, whose avowed purpose was "simply to kill" the "dinks and slopes." Sent on a night patrol to a village, they surprised some Viet Cong smoking and talking by water well. Undetected, they fired from a distance, killed them all, and quickly came back to the base. Elated and proud the men were eager to tell their comrades what the patrol had accomplished. One soldier was in rapture as he recounted it. The enemies "were right out there, right in the open, right in the middle of the village, in a little clearing, just sitting on their asses! Shit, I almost shit! Ten of them, just sitting there. Jesus, we gave them hell. Damn, we gave it to them!" His face was on fire in the night, his teeth were flashing as he paced back and forth, incapable of containing his joy as his anxiety diminished. Then he asked his lieutenant to show the trophy, of which he was very proud, an ear which had been cut off one of the enemy's heads. [101] The killing had a cathartic effect on the men. More than eliminating enemies; it eliminated their gloom. After the exploit, an extraordinary euphoria overtakes them. They had done to the enemy what they expected the enemy to do to them. Temporarily, their death anxiety disappeared, and having been relieved of a burden, they became cheerful and happy. It was a personal deed—the pleasure of sighting the enemy unaware, the pleasure in killing them easily, and the immense relief that this cowardly act gave them.

For one helicopter gunner, killing the enemy had become an obsession. His performance was a self-confidence-building affair which he regarded highly. Expecting a reporter to do a story on him, he boasted: "I am so fucking good... Got me one hundred and fifty-seven gooks killed. And fifty caribous." And he assured the reporter that "them're all certified."[102] The death that constantly threatened him and everyone else had been deflected—turned against those that would be dealing it out. His pride had little to do with the safety of his unit or with winning the war. Even desecration of the dead served to placate death anxiety. Violence to the dead revealed an exceptional thirst for stamping out the constant fear that gripped them, a fear of the unknown lurking in the jungle shadows, or of being recipients of similar desecrations from the enemy. The resulting fear and unease caused Americans to respond in obnoxious ways, such as urinating on the enemy dead. Lieutenant Puller, who witnessed this kind of abuse failed to understand the motive and was shocked. The sergeant who buried the body while the lieutenant was in shock told him that he "would soon understand." [103] What was he supposed to understand? Possibly, this very personal and sick form of hostility had a cathartic effect. It compensated for the Americans' inability to come to grips with an enemy that was invisible and everywhere. A captain firing an M-16 on full automatic on a pile of enemy corpses was animated by an antagonism that turned him into a monster. When he had finished, he revealed a face that "was flushed and mottled and twisted like he had his face skin on inside out... he looked like he had had a heart attack out there. His eyes were rolled up half into his head, his mouth was sprung open, and his tongue was out, but he was smiling." [104] The extraordinary personal satisfaction derived from violence to the dead was prompted, not by any immediate military circumstance, but by the release of tension—of living constantly on the edge of death.

The death of friends and comrades added to the soldiers' anxiety and became a common and powerful reason for killing. It was both a personal and satisfying affair for a Marine unit who by painful humping was trying to reach the Demilitarized Zone. After a successful ambush "killing was unbelievably easy." The North Vietnamese either cowered in terror as their boyish faces were shot point blank, or they turned and ran up the barren slopes a few steps before having their backs and legs shattered by American bullets. It was great fun for the Marines even though "the bounds of reason were being crossed" that morning. "It was like practicing up for the range," one Marine explained, "we had got some from the prone position, then the sitting, from one knee, standing up. Hell, it was easier than the damn range!" Some felt they could not get enough; others wanted to carve initials on the chests of the dead. Only a few were repulsed by a killing that "was too easy." As one result of that massacre, the chance to take prisoners and possibly save American lives in the future was wasted. But for the Marines, the performance held a great deal of value. They were getting even for the pain the enemy had inflicted on them and all soldiers in the course of the campaign. "There was a beautiful vengeance in it all: the thousands of grunts who had stepped on all the box mines and booby traps and pungi stakes in the past five years had died like this too. Without the chance to fight back."[105] Finally, this unbridled killing had relieved them of great weight.

 Because it was sanctioned by the war, they killed without regret or pangs of conscience. When Lieutenant Hodges's patrol failed to carry out the ambush he had planned, he felt defeated and depressed, "They got us again. They got us. He hated it and he hated himself." One of his men lost a leg, another his fingers. Hodges felt that he and his soldiers were nothing but a "floating islet waiting to be killed." But then the prospect of attacking the enemy raised his spirit. "A surge of deep, undirected anger and desire to kill," overtook him. On another occasion, when a contingent of Vietnamese was about to be ambushed by his troops, he rejoiced at the prospect of destroying them unaware. He "felt joy and anticipation so hard to contain that he found himself bobbing up and down inside the trench where he hid... Come on! Ten more meters and you die."[106] Americans wanted revenge, regardless of the military mandate. The recollection of a veteran nurse explained Hodges's joy, "All my hatred for the Vietnamese and my wanting to kill them was really a reflection of the pain that I had felt seeing those young men die and hurt."[107] Pain and suffering had broken the equilibrium of the inner self, and revenge was the only way to restore it. This was the sentiment of a nurse trained to save lives who had to handle too many mangled soldiers.

UNDER FIRE

Coming under fire was a frightening experience. The air was like poisonous gas and seemed composed of pieces of lead "flying at two-thousand miles an hour."[108] Some soldiers under fire slumped and cowered, terrorized by the impending destruction. "You writhe like a man suddenly waking in the middle of a heart transplant," one veteran recorded.[109] Others were gripped by an overwhelming impulse to respond. They came alive with an intense resolve to kill. If he first overcame the shock of the event, such as a paralyzing fear, coming under fire would unleash a soldier's fury in a torrent of energy. But this, too, was purely a personal response. It impelled the combatant "to move, to face and to overcome the danger." One lieutenant found extraordinary energy and resolve within himself. "An eerie sense of calm came over me," he recalls, "my mind was working with a speed and clarity" which were exceptional. He felt as dangerous as a "cornered animal... terrified and every instinct in him focused on a single end: destroying the thing that frightens him." Isolated from any idea or ideals, his fear was fueled not from a belief in a cause, but by this unusual state of being—senses quickened, consciousness sharpened. It was something "like the elevated state of awareness induced by drugs." Transformed into a vehicle of destruction, he "seemed to live more intensely."[110] In the heat of battle the natural, instinctual mind lives in the moment alone, and much of the knowledge regarding military tactics and maneuvering gained in training flies out the window. But the recruits are also taught to defend themselves by killing without compunction or compassion. This is the residue when the civilized mind fails. Such was the state under fire in Vietnam. With bestial strength and vigor, they killed automatically and efficiently. "You are fast and graceful, a green jungle cat" and feel and act "like a god" while you scream at the enemy: "Die! Die!"[111] This feeling translated into an action that found its supreme expression in the killing. Another reporter who was close to the combatants summed up the experience, "It would take you out of your head and your body too." What soldiers called courage, the will to attack and dispatch the enemy came after an incredible surge of "undifferentiated energy cut loose by the intensity of the moment, a mind loss that sent the actor on an incredible run." No effort was made to gauge the strength of the enemy or plan a tactic that would enable him to prevail. Under fire, his psychic balance was broken, and he performed deeds he would never think of doing otherwise.[112] Emotion alone could lead them to kill profusely and efficiently, and deeds that might be called more murderous than heroic were performed. A lieutenant leading a platoon up a hill under fire that was kept from reaching a village at the top recorded the response of the men under his command, "It was a collective emotional detonation of men who had been pushed to the extremity of endurance." They suddenly became very violent, quickly "turning into vandals." Yet, they accomplished a successful counterattack. They advanced irresistibly, drove the enemy out of the village, and whooping like savages, rampaged through yet another village, torching huts, setting the whole place aflame, and tossing grenades into cement houses that could not be burnt. Some of the people were torched by soldiers who had turned into arsonists. Their frenzy made them efficient destroyers with no more feeling for themselves or others. Nevertheless, the platoon accomplished what a disciplined unit unmotivated by rage would not have been able to do—the complete destruction of a village and its inhabitants. It had nothing to do with applying the right military tactic or securing advantage for the unit. Rather, it was for the Americans a personal victory over the frustration and fear that had held them tense for months prior. "We had relieved our own pain by inflicting it on others," the lieutenant summed up the result of his unit's operation.[113] Revenge was sweet.

A helicopter assault on a hot landing zone usually placed the combatant under fire in a unique way and triggered a singular impulse to kill. The enclosed space, the noise, the speed, and the exposure to enemy fire made it one of the worst experiences for soldiers fighting in Vietnam and created a state of being far more tense and frightening than a ground assault. "On the ground, an infantryman has some control over his destiny or at least the illusion of it. In a helicopter under fire, he hasn't even the illusion," a participant in helicopter assaults recalled. He lived with the feeling of being trapped and powerless until a blind rage to be on the ground firing overcame him. All he could think of was the moment when he could escape the machine and release his tension. All other considerations—the rights and wrongs of an action, impending victory or defeat, the battle's aim or its absence—became irrelevant. In this state, the combatant was so absorbed in venting his rage that all other concerns disappeared in his zeal to kill.[114]

PSYCHOTIC BREAKDOWN OR GOING BERSERK

It is understandable that the violent and traumatic experience of being under fire enjoined an equally violent response of the soldiers. But there were far less violent experiences that generated an extraordinary drive to kill. The battlefield climate itself created a singular state of mind, that could upset a man's inner balance and release an unrestrained impulse to kill. It was what some veterans elegantly called a sickness, a form of insanity that was far from rare. A veteran recalled, "In Vietnam, you are mad all the time—you wake up mad—you are mad when you eat, and mad when you sleep, mad when you walk, mad when you sit—just mad all the time." Vietnam made men cynical and despairing, and some "just went insane, followed the black-light arrow around the bend and took possession of the madness that had been waiting there in trust for them." Craziness appeared to be common enough. The soldiers spoke openly about it. "Going crazy was built into the tour," a reporter noted, fearfully adding that "the best you could hope for was that it did not happen around you." But it happened quite frequently and unexpectedly, too: "Everyone knew grunts who'd gone crazy in the middle of a firefight, gone crazy on patrol, gone crazy back at camp, gone crazy during rest periods, and gone crazy one month after they had returned home."[115] This sickness naturally turned killing into a project dictated by a personal state of being, not duty.

An infantry lieutenant revealed to his brother in 1968 that to him killing human beings was the same as killing animals. "I get all excited when I see a VC," he wrote in a letter, "just like when I see a deer. I go ape firing at him. It isn't that I am so crazy... Civilians think that such thinking is crazy, but it is no big deal. He runs, you fire." But his motivation and performance troubled him, for on the same day he sent that letter, he wrote again to another man to confess that a sickness held him in thrall, and he liked it. He wrote again to his brother, "I have actually enjoyed some of the things I have done which would be repulsive to a healthy mind. This place makes you sick in the head. When one starts to enjoy the sickness of war, he is sick."[116]

Once the viciousness that ruled the battlefield repeatedly touched the soldiers, they became "war-washed" that is, hardened. Compassion, if they had any, disappeared, and their propensity to kill grew. They became cynical and despairing and found that killing was a way out of their funk. For some "only heavy killing could make them feel so alive." They passed beyond callousness into savagery, which opened the door to insanity. Some became so engrossed in killing that they "just went insane" every time they went into combat. When the killing frenzy seized them, it was a permit to mania. Combat was fertile ground for insanity. Almost every combatant "snapped over the line at least once."[117] As a consequence, combat was sometimes cherished for the simple reason that it gave a soldier license to cross all boundaries where their lust for vengeance made it easy to face the enemy and enjoy killing. This psychotic break gained value among many and made them proud of their accomplishments. A Marine remembers himself and his comrades who served at Da Nang in 1966 going out of their minds in combat and, as a result, killing, not just the enemy, but everyone. "We were crazy, but it is built into the culture," the Marine explained. In combat, it was "like institutionalized insanity. You can do basically what you want... You can get away with murder. And the beautiful thing about the military is, there is always somebody that can serve up as a scapegoat." [118] Insanity was a way of soldiering. A Navy Seal, who would become assistant dean of students at one of the University of California campuses, recalled his own state of mind and behavior and that of his comrades: "We didn't make much distinction about who the enemy was." Making a distinction was impossible, because "all you were supposed to do over there was be crazy... so we were crazy." And being crazy "wasn't something we turned on and off, at least not for me. I was insane the entire time I was in Vietnam." Craziness set the Navy Seals apart from ordinary soldiers. The ordinary soldier produced an inferior performance, which disqualified him from even discussing or judging the Navy Seals' behavior. On the other hand, the Seals' exceptional performance legitimized crimes prompted by their craziness. One of them confessed, "The off-times were just as insane as the on-duty times. We'd get in fights and blow Army bases up. I went out and sold every [military] truck I could get my hands on." Insanity simplified and legitimized crime and killing. "We were killing people out in the field that I had no bad feeling about at all, so if you are back to an Army area or whatever, and those guys aren't going out in the field as much as you under that kind of exposure, and you can handle whatever comes down, you are not going to put up with shit from anybody." Sadly, the craziness did not leave the Seals when they left Vietnam. Apparently, no effort was made by the military to re-integrate them into civilian life on their return to the U.S. Their instincts were completely anti-social, even murderous. The military had succeeded in producing efficient fighting men, at the cost of creating psychopaths unfit for civilized life. They were a danger to themselves and their families. When they got back to the United States, one of them recalled, all the commanders could think of doing was "to lock us all up in a bunch of big boxes." They said "'We don't know what to do with you guys.'" Back home the Seals quarreled and fought with the police, beat up gangs, jumped off piers, and did all kinds of "insane things."[119] Skillful killing and destruction were their hallmarks. Their recklessness had been validated by the war and could not be easily turned off.

"Going berserk" was a spectacular and stark form of insanity. The Viet Congs' abuses both of the dead and the living hit the soldiers hard. However, even less dramatic events such as the death of a friend, and being wounded, overrun, surrounded, or trapped could drive a soldier mad. One or another of these incidents would upset his mental and emotional balance, and he would become possessed by an overwhelming need to find and hurt the enemy. A typical berserk combatant confessed, "Everybody gets hit, and the hate builds up, especially seeing what they did to guys in the outfit they got hold of—cut off their dicks, cut off their ears." As the enemy's atrocities increased, this combatant's psychosis mushroomed. He "really loved fucking killing" so much that "he could not get enough." It soothed his pain; he felt better with every Vietnamese he could kill. Another combatant who saw his close friend destroyed by a land mine had a sudden, wild crisis, "And I cried, and I cried, and I cried... And I stopped crying. And probably did not cry again for twenty years. I turned. I had no feelings." In the meantime, a violent impulse got hold of him, "I wanted to hurt. I wanted to hurt. And I wanted to hurt." Yet another combatant after a similar experience was seized by a raging thirst for revenge: "It consumed my mind. It consumed my body. It consumed every part of me." It was now imperative to kill the enemy. But though he did a lot of killing, he remained unsatisfied, "I couldn't get enough. I could have had my hands around ten Gooks' throats a day, and it wouldn't be enough."[120]

As previously discussed, coming under fire could unleash a torrent of energy and exceptional strength. Likewise, these combatants drew their martial spirit and surplus strength from a primitive, instinctual self without regard to any ideal or cause. If one excludes the personal emotion of revenge, one could say they approximated Clausewitz's theory of the ideal soldier, one free of political and ethical prejudices, untouched by fear, and totally absorbed in the task of killing. On another occasion, when a helicopter was shot down and the soldiers, paralyzed by fear, refused to fire their weapons, one man suddenly had a third psychotic break. He alone stood up and began firing, oblivious of the enemy and the risk: "I felt like a god, this power flowing through me. Anybody could have picked me off there—but I was untouchable." [121] The heedless action of this soldier and others like him are related neither to winning a battle, to military duty, nor to the love of country. They needed to vent their rage and conquer fear. Emotion overwhelmed them, and internal forces were unleashed that caused them to perform deeds in defiance of all moral restraint. In spite of their going crazy, to the extent that they succeeded in killing the enemy, their deeds were honored. The commanders came to value them as the best in the business and often recognized and rewarded them as heroes.

In Vietnam, there existed thousands of albums made up of plastic pages each containing pictures of enemy corpses or parts of them. Severed-head shots, show a head resting on the chest of a dead man or being held up by a smiling Marine. Many were arranged in rows with burning cigarettes in their mouths, their eyes open. There were photos of Viet Cong suspects being dragged in the dust by trucks or being hung by their heels at various spots in some jungle clearing, of Marines, holding one or two ears or a whole necklace made of ears, called "love beads." These pictures, which were among the Marines' favorite keepsakes, were meant to be trophies and testimonials of their prowess. It was as though civilization had regressed to an earlier time when vengeance and cruelty toward adversaries were the norms. All civilized boundaries were crossed.[122]

WEAPONRY

Americans could claim superior weaponry on the battlefield. A veteran who had experienced the mental and practical aspects of dispatching the adversary discussed the role of a weapon in the hand of a soldier. "You drop someone in hell," he recounted, "and give him a gun and tell him to kill for some goddamned amorphous reason he can't even articulate. Then suddenly he feels an emotion that makes utter sense, and he has a gun in his hand, and he has seen dead people for months and the reasons are irrelevant anyway, so pow. And it's utterly logical because the emotion was right." [123] Gun in hand and passion in heart are the explosive ingredients. There is no thought of tactics or military objectives. What matters is the power of a gun in the hand. Thus, if a simple gun so easily can facilitate the killing impulse, far more powerful weapons can create an even greater sense of power. "Nothing finer" than shooting from a helicopter, a gunship pilot revealed, "You are up there at two thousand, you are God, just open up the flexies and watch it pee, nail those slime to the paddy wall, nothing finer."[124] The immense power of modern weaponry bolstered the soldier's confidence and enhanced his aggressive will. The means of destruction thrilled Lieutenant Broyles. Having fired a bazooka or an M-60 machine gun, he realized at once that he held tremendous power. Those weapons were like having "a magic sword, a soldier's Excalibur," that could cause a truck or a house to disappear "in a blast of sound and energy and light." [125] Francis Coppola tapped into the sinister pleasure of this destructive power in his film, Apocalypse Now. Lt. Col. William Kilgore (Robert Duval) turns on Wagner's Ride of the Valkyries full blast on his radio while leading his helicopter unit in a murderous raid on a coastal village as the villagers try in vain to flee a fiery death. He embodies the insane fury of the enterprise with his comment, "I love the smell of napalm in the morning." Some soldiers were so infatuated by the weapons they wielded that they experienced a kind of second life. "A gun is power," a veteran explained. Carrying a gun was like having "a permanent hard-on. It was a pure sexual trip every time you got to pull the trigger." [126] Their elite weapons enabled Americans to do a lot of killing, but in the end, proved useless for military purposes. They went against the belief that military power is the solution to political or ideological differences. Ironically, they were a sign of weakness. For it could only be construed as an admission of political failure that the United States had to resort to high-tech weapons such as helicopters and plant-killing chemicals to confront a revolutionary force that was far inferior in armament. Headquarters might have asked itself why it needed special forces, the best commandos armed with the very best means of warfare to fight an enemy that was short of expert training, modern weaponry, and firepower. The obvious, but unacknowledged answer is that it would take "all the technical proficiency our system [could] provide to make up for the woeful lack of popular support and political savvy of most of the regimes that the West has thus far sought to prop up."[127]

The North Vietnamese people had a powerful and deeply felt commitment that sustained the Viet Cong's ability to inflict on Americans a surprisingly high number of casualties. They had no tanks and no air power, but on their native soil, they were defending their land and culture. They desired with every fiber of their being to drive the Americans out of their country. "There was joy in eluding our patrols, joy in setting ambushes, joy in infiltrating our bases and destroying our tanks and riverboats. And that joy was magnified because Americans appeared so invulnerable." Against such a cause Americans could not compete. The thrill that fighting gave to an ex-Viet Cong, whom the retired Lieutenant Broyles met on a return trip to Vietnam in 1984, was unknown to American combatants. For the Northerners, this war was the "transcendent challenge." Their actions were driven by patriotism. American actions, on the other hand, bore the marks of men who killed because "that power in your finger, the soft, seductive touch of the trigger," was there, asking him to experience his "physical and emotional limits," as if he were in "a game, a brutal, deadly game" that tested individual courage and endurance, regardless of military victory.[128]

THE INVISIBLE ENEMY

Neither could American weaponry make up for the inferiority of their commanders' military strategy. The Americans tried to offset the Viet Cong's ability to make itself invisible; they tried to do this with the indiscriminate killing of suspected enemies. The problem was "you couldn't find the enemy," an enlisted soldier in the field recalled.[129] The enemy was adept at ambushing Americans. Land mines, sniper fire, and mortars killed or maimed them, both in the jungle and in the villages. Still, the enemy was nowhere to be seen. Its secrecy tormented the foreign invaders. The Viet Cong were so successful in striking and hiding that the Americans suffered more casualties from booby traps, mines, and sniper fire than from actual combat. Military action often came down to trying to force them into the open. In one tragicomic flashback a veteran recalled that the men of his unit did everything they could think of to flush out the enemy, but in vain, "They killed a water buffalo. They burned rice and shot chickens and scattered jugs of grain. They trampled paddies. Tore up fences. Dumped dirt into wells, diverted ditches, provoked madness. But they could not drive the enemy into showing itself, and the silence was exhausting." These same soldiers went through villages along the Song Tra Bong River, surrounded them, searched them, and sometimes burned them down, but they "never saw the living enemy." The hidden opponents rendered the war aimless—no targets and "nothing to shoot back at." And while the enemy disappeared into the night, into tunnels, paddies, and bamboo groves, or into the elephant grass, it was eminently successful in killing Americans.[130] The mine explosions were the all too visible signs of their unseen presence. Americans suffered symptoms of paranoia. They could not "feel safe anywhere in this whole country."[131]

The Viet Cong's invisible presence was more harmful than its real presence. It created among the Americans marching through elephant grass a mind-altering fear; they were convinced that everywhere men were around who "desperately [wanted] to kill you." And they were right. Their adversaries were everywhere. In every village, there were Viet Cong sympathizers not necessarily actively engaged in hostilities. Even if these escaped the direct violence of the war, they recognized a foreign invader who neither spoke their language nor respected their culture. Nor would they sympathize with the South Vietnamese troops because, after all, it was essentially a civil war. Indeed, the North Vietnamese cause was pervasive in the hearts of many local peasants. In this atmosphere, American paranoia multiplied, and the soldiers rapidly aged.[132] Moreover, the knowledge that they were fighting a mysterious and unbeatable enemy, intensified their savagery. Americans yearned to face the enemy in a pitched battle; it was a naive hope. The Viet Cong had no intention of confronting them head-on, as they had done decisively with the French at Dien Bien Phu in 1954. Their strategy was to hit and run, to materialize suddenly out of the undergrowth and to melt as quickly back into it. The intent, always deadly, was to keep the Americans on edge, to intensify fear, and as the preceding quotations have shown, it worked. In contemporary Pentagonese, this was asymmetrical warfare. The success of the Viet Cong over the soldiers of the most powerful army in the world was a disturbing realization. Since the American yearning for a pitched battle was impossible to satisfy, they began to invent the enemy wherever they went, and since it was difficult to distinguish friend from foe, they often killed Vietnamese indiscriminately. This carelessness was seconded by the disposition already noted, that killing became necessary for overcoming one's own death anxiety.[133] We never knew which of the Vietnamese "was our enemy and which our friend," a veteran recalled. This gave rise to the opinion that anyone could be an enemy, and easy to conclude that "everyone" was an enemy.

[134] The Vietnamese soldiers were very different from the antagonists of past wars. In World War II and Korea, the enemy was readily identified, openly attacked, and fought defensively. But in Vietnam, the enemy was elusive, mysterious, and not in uniform. In the American imagination, he was "a bogey man" with terrible powers, rising out of the earth. The primitive but successful methods that the Viet Cong adopted in the face of American technology made them that much more formidable. As a result, the Americans fought a "darkness" they could neither penetrate nor understand.[135] Eventually, the darkness no longer mattered, because the hidden enemy was brought into the daylight of the soldier's imagination. When this happened, the invention fostered the propensity to attack and kill anyone suspected of being an enemy. That darkness and the need to invent the enemy were magnified by the difficulty in communicating with the Vietnamese people. The language barrier and the American's ignorance of their culture fostered hostility. Not knowing the language, the Americans did not know the people, and not knowing the people, they could not tell friends from enemies and could not know whom to trust. The lack of trust was lethal.[136] The racial difference, too, was a dark wall. In Vietnam racism was overt and damaging. One could see changes happening in soldiers who would not have dreamed of calling an Oriental a "gook" or "slope head" in the U.S.[137] But, far from home and in a strange country, they became resentful, frustrated, and insulting. The Vietnamese were regarded as worthless gooks against whom it was legitimate to use violence. To some grunts, murder, rape, or any form of harassment of unarmed civilians somehow constituted an expression of masculinity. There was even a lingering suspicion that an American soldier who refused to take part in abusing the Vietnamese was less than a man. Atrocities became part of the killing. After the third month of a tour of duty, savagery was a reality for every soldier. "Hell," one grunt rationalized with an extraordinary sense of impunity, "we figure we could be dead the next minute or day anyhow so what the fuck difference does it make what we do? What difference does it make if we shoot at farmers in their paddies or screw village girls? Who would give a shit?" They killed for the most unjustifiable and inhuman reasons in the world. After all, the grunt's rationalization went on, "it did not look like the Vietnamese

would be losing much if they were robbed, belted around a little or killed." This was the kind of violence the commanders tolerated. Americans were not greeted as liberators by the Vietnamese like their fathers had been in Europe. A grunt felt unappreciated by the very people he had been sent to help. He felt that his sacrifices and deprivations were not valued and that he ought to make the people pay for their ingratitude.[138] The killings multiplied, but American offensive actions secured no major victory and were sometimes even harmful. In 1966 a Marine platoon leader called one Search and Destroy operation "very successful," when the Americans managed to kill "a few probably innocent civilians."[139] Soldiers and commanders came to believe without any supporting evidence that all Vietnamese were the enemy. Even in the United States, war supporters believed that the Vietnamese, especially in the countryside, were potential enemies. "We are fighting an entire people," one of them declared, and "since everyone in the countryside of Vietnam is to a lesser or greater degree our potential enemy, it is perfectly logical to kill everyone in sight."[140] Instead of becoming more cautious, the dubious identity of the Vietnamese redoubled the eagerness of Americans to kill them, perhaps because it was less time-consuming than being selective, or perhaps they believed that the haphazard killing would eliminate more enemies. The American forces ended up fighting the entire country.[141] The convenient belief that all Vietnamese were Viet Cong created a readily identifiable enemy. But if fighting the whole country was an illusion, the strengthening of resolve to kill as many as possible was a reality. Americans picked their adversaries with neither discrimination nor reason, so long as they could eliminate uncertainty and placate their anxiety. Killing the imagined enemy was standard practice. One combatant was commended and rewarded for killing nine men that his superiors chose to define as "soldiers." In fact, he confessed later that there were more than nine, and probably a few enemies, "I think I killed more than that. But like I say, we were going into the village, somebody I don't like... I shoot them down. But they had written up that it was combat, heavy combat... If there wasn't an enemy out there," some combatants "made it be the enemy." Not knowing one from another, killing anybody was justified in American eyes, "You can't tell who's your enemy. You got to shoot kids."[142]

BODY COUNT

As if Headquarters meant to sanction and strengthen Americans' penchant for killing, it issued a directive called "Body Count." It was designed on the premise that the larger the number of enemies killed, the weaker the enemy would become, and the more measurable the success of American forces. The units in the field were to keep a careful count of the dead. They were also expected to show high body counts, not just because dead bodies proved American success, but also because they proved that the strategy decided upon by the High Command was the right one. However, the body count was a self-defeating strategy, for when the number was high, it generated the illusion that the war was being won when in fact the enemy had a large number of men in reserve, and their losses left only a small dent. Not only was it hard to count the bodies in the field (accuracy was out of the question), but it encouraged the indiscriminate killing of Vietnamese, as anyone could be counted as an enemy. Moreover, it indulged the desire of those soldiers who wanted to get even at all costs and prompted some units to inflate the number to show success. It led Americans to kill people who were neither Viet Cong nor North Vietnamese. They were "looking to kill" every time they went on a search and destroy mission. [143] All that mattered from the top to the commanders on the field was the body count. And "the killing thing seeped down into every rifleman." Some units were given a quota for the week, and if they did not get it, they were just sent out again. "Just killing made it all very simple, and the simplicity made it all very professional. Everyone knew the job—even the dumbest kid." [144] The directive turned out to be an "infamous measurement of success." But headquarters stuck to the body count even though it made every combatant a bounty hunter and a liar. [145] One young captain disclosed to a news reporter that his superior had changed the content of the declaration he had made about his activities in the field, "I went out and killed one Viet Cong and liberated a prisoner," he related. "Next day the major called me in and told me that I had killed fourteen VC and liberated six prisoners." He showed the medal that testified to this fabrication. [146] No matter the errors and distortions, the officers placed a great deal of value on the number of bodies, and some, who had become "obsessed with the body count," wanted a count that would satisfy headquarters, even though they knew that the count was a lie. However, not everyone was comfortable. General Westmoreland declared that he had nothing to do with it and implicitly repudiated it, at least in words. He "abhorred the term" so much, he wrote in *A Soldier Reports,* that he burst into cursing every time he heard it. He ascribed the coining and use of the term to unspecified "others," declaring that he saw no point in trying to modify it since it had become established in the language of war. [147] But he did nothing to stop the practice, which continued methodically. For students of this war, the practice became the "perfect symbol of America's descent into evil," fusing the essential soul-numbing, brutalization, and illusion "into a grotesque technicalization." [148] The body count was, above all, the perfect symbol for the activity the soldiers came to cherish more than any other. Counting bodies suited their emotional need while conforming to the logic instilled in their training. It especially fit the instructions given to the Marines who were eminently suited to perform killing by virtue of their training which was to make killing the supreme purpose of service on the battlefield. Their trainers apparently embraced Clausewitz's warning that belief in a cause would hinder prowess. They were trained to bring out the primitive instinct to kill, to make themselves fearless and aggressive. It came down to "a boot-camp deification of killing," with the charge "to be brave," "to fight well," and "to kill people." The Marines were destined to be "professional killers in the service of the United States government." [149] One Marine in the field surmised that his training had the purpose of instilling contempt for human life and nourishing the instinct to destroy it. He thought it twisted the concept and practice of military duty, that ambushing the enemy, for example, was peddled not as a smart, successful tactic, but encouraged as plain murder, "Ambushes are murder as animals." A good Marine turned himself into a "minister of death, praying for war." Training murder is fun." [150] Military duty was reduced to murder and murder to pleasure, and no matter how repugnant the duty, it had to be fulfilled. If a recruit disobeyed an order during basic training, a witness at Lieutenant Calley's court-martial revealed, he would be hit over the head and kicked in the chest. He was trained to obey his officers blindly. "If an officer tells you to go out and stand on your head in the middle of the highway, you do it." [151] Generally, the training erased the truth learned at home that human life is precious and the taking of it wrong, but this did not take hold in a healthy proportion of the recruits. Respect for human life survived, and many Marines felt degraded by the duty to kill by the standard set by the body count. Lieutenant Robert Santos, the highest decorated veteran from the state of New York, wrote that his responsibility was to kill and be good at it. He did his best, but eventually realized that to enjoy a high body and high kill ratio was "a fucking way to live your life."

To stress the value of the body count and to keep up a high rate of killing, a public display of corpses was sometimes arranged. The dead would be piled up, and the Quartermaster Corps would call in the newsmen, NBC or CBS. One soldier scoffed at the propaganda and public relations aspect of it, "They wasn't out there when we was shooting, but they was out there when it was over for the body count."[152] The general wanted the dead collected outside the morgue and left where they were in the open even though he knew that in a short time the stench would be unbearable. He wanted them to be seen by the new officers. It was vital that they "get used to the sight of blood," he said, and the evidence thus displayed would verify the success of American arms.[153] If training failed to convert the soldier to the religion of death, the body count helped them see the light. "Our mission," one lieutenant understood very well, "was not to win terrain or seize positions, but simply to kill: to kill Communists and to kill as many as possible."[154] The official demand put pressure on commanders and their units to produce corpses.[155] Some commanders even gave extra beer rations and time off to those who killed a confirmed Viet Cong. [156] The troops complied with the directive, often producing corpses of neither North Vietnamese nor Viet Cong. Those that excelled in body counts possessed neither discipline nor patriotism. Their propensity to kill demonstrated that "one of the most brutal things in the world is your average nineteen-year-old American boy."[157] Instilled with the "spirit of the bayonet," malleable youngsters were turned into mindless killers who regarded their actions, not as evil but as proof of their valor.[158] They recorded their kills with notches on their rifles and the corpses as "evidence of a warrior's prowess."[159] But the killing scarred them for life. Eventually, they became victims of lives that were devastated by what they had done.

MY LAI

What happened at My Lai in March 1968 was the consequence of the previous combat experience of Lieutenant Calley's unit. It had suffered losses from an enemy it could not see. The losses and the inability to confront the enemy fueled their determination to massacre the entire inhabitants of My Lai. An unnamed soldier who was there at the time recalls, "You are in Vietnam, and they are using real bullets... Here in Vietnam, they are actually shooting people for no reason... Here you can go ahead and shoot them for nothing. As a matter of fact, it is even smiled upon, you know. Good for you." The battlefield atmosphere and the killing field were the air everyone breathed, and to many involved, the slaughter was not unnatural. In retrospect, the above-quoted soldier realized that "everything" was "backward,"[160] but at the time, he had neither the thought nor the strength to restrain his actions. The killing had become routine. Supported by the belief that all Vietnamese were at least sympathizers, he assumed it was his duty, and he was absorbed by it.

The combatants at My Lai and other places where atrocities were perpetrated have admitted that in killing old men, women, and children, they believed at the time that they had "engaged the enemy—had finally got it to stand up and fight." [161] The American division that devastated My Lai, believed the villagers were the enemy. Lieutenant Calley's court-martial disclosed that on the day of the massacre, Captain Medina and Calley brought up the question of the enemy's identity. According to them the unit who had entered the village wanted to fight instead of marching around and "getting blown up" by booby traps and mines. Medina supported the troops' need to kill. He gave the troops the impression that they "could kill the people, could kill anybody they saw," and he identified the enemy by defining it, "Anybody who was running from us, hiding from us, or who appeared to be the enemy." He told them that if a man was running, they should "shoot him," and that if a woman with a rifle was running, they should also "shoot her." Medina in fact told his troops "to go in rapidly and neutralize everything. To kill everything." Asked by his troops if he meant "women and children, too," he replied:

"I mean everything." [162] At the court-martial, Pvt. Paul Meadlo, who had witnessed the massacre, testified that the children, women, and men that Calley ordered to be rounded up, were suspected "of being Viet Cong," and when the prosecutor asked Calley what his men were firing at as they swept through the village, he replied that they were firing at "the enemy," All living Vietnamese in the village were held to be enemies. As the prosecutor tried to better identify those people, he managed to get Calley to admit that they were "human beings." To justify his refusal to identify those human beings more precisely, Calley replied, "I didn't discriminate between individuals in the village, sir. They were all the enemy, they were all to be destroyed, sir."[163]

The men of the unit that raided My Lai were disheartened and restless when they came into the village. The killing compensated them for the deaths their unit had suffered earlier. After the massacre, they felt better. None who took part in it placed it in the context of the American cause for going to Vietnam. Some revealed reasons which were obviously personal. One said: "Until now we were dying uselessly." The fact that they were dying with hardly ever having the chance to confront the enemy, generated an indiscriminate will to kill. [164] My Lai was a case of displaced anger. As victims may turn into abusers, Pvt. Meadlo revealed the reason for the killings, "We were supposed to get satisfaction from this village for all the men we had lost." The private really believed this; he killed without compunction or discrimination. George Latimer, a lawyer defending Calley at his court-martial, asked Meadlo, "You killed men, women, and children?" Meadlo replied, "Yes."[165]

"My Lai was largely a product of the numerical ambition of high-level officers,"[166] that is, of their pressure on troops to kill as many Viet Cong, real or imagined, as possible. The deeds of twenty-four-year-old Lieutenant Calley and his unit dramatically combined in a single frame the directive to search and destroy. At his court-martial, Calley said that Captain Medina, his direct superior, "would put in the highest acceptable body count that he could." The desire to be credited with killing ran high and "everybody wanted their companies to have the highest count."[167] Just prior to My Lai, an entire squad had been destroyed by a booby trap. An enemy had to be found to pay the price. As the soldiers approached My Lai the order went out "to kill everything in the village." It was an opportunity for revenge on a people (perhaps sympathetic to the enemy) for losses suffered earlier, and the troops interpreted the order to mean "kill every man, woman, and child in the village." Captain Medina, gave his men the impression they "could kill the people . . . anybody they saw."[168] Thus, psyched for killing, the shooting started almost as a chain reaction, and a high body count—347 bodies, including old men, women, and children was the result. In the end, only three weapons were discovered, a sign that the people represented no danger to the Americans who had ostensibly come to search them. Lieutenant Calley explained that there was "a lot of stress on body counts" and every company "was competing with body counts, everybody wanted their companies to have the highest body count." The body count was regarded as a smart and useful strategy, and often the mantle of heroism was placed on the shoulders of the killers. At the end of his trial, Calley was transformed by a good section of the American population into "a hero of our time."[169] Killing the largest number of people became the main thrust of the American strategy for winning the war. When it seemed that the enemy could not be identified, everyone became the enemy, and the reason for killing gained plausibility and urgency. "You can't tell who's your enemy. You got to shoot kids, you got to shoot women."[170]

Until the massacre at My Lai was exposed, most of the atrocities that occurred in Vietnam were disregarded or covered up. Vietnamese sources have since "detailed hundreds of massacres and large-scale operations that resulted in thousands of civilian deaths, but those reports were dismissed out of hand as communist propaganda."[171] When a large part of the American public turned Lieutenant Calley and his unit's widespread, indiscriminate slaughter into a heroic performance, a high rate of killing came to be recognized as a heroic deed. Many spectators at Fort Benning and millions of Americans elsewhere who had followed the trial in the media proclaimed him "not a murderer of the innocent but a hero—a hero of our time." Instead of being recognized for what he was—the murderer of unresisting, unarmed, innocent old men, women, children, and babies—Calley was transformed into "the symbol of the American soldier in the world—a hero." [172] In the aftermath, General Westmoreland sent a message of congratulations to the officers and men of Calley's company "for outstanding action."[173] The idea and practice of indiscriminate killing were raised to the highest rank of military virtue by the policy of the body count; thus, it was logical that the commanding general would praise a performance that produced an enormous number of dead in less than a day. Though the general refrained from explicitly calling the troops heroes, the troops considered themselves heroes. Indeed, later discussions and interviews conducted by psychiatrists with My Lai veterans showed that some were recreating My Lai in their imagination "as if it were a great battle and a noble victory and themselves as all-powerful warrior-heroes who had magnificently carried out their ordeal."[174]

SURVIVAL

Eventually, the murderous instinct came to satisfy a need more pressing than that imposed by either the body count or revenge on an enemy. When American soldiers realized that victory was impossible and their sacrifices useless, killing Vietnamese for the sake of their own survival became the most sane and vital goal. Personal survival eventually became the cause of Americans in Vietnam, "The only thing the grunts found to win in Vietnam was 365 consecutive days of life."[175] Although in the fall of 1965 the war was still in its beginning stage, the soldiers already fought and killed "for no cause other than [their] own survival," and many were made ruthless toward the enemy by an "overpowering greed for survival."[176] It encouraged the combatant to kill as many enemies as he could, soldiers or other Vietnamese viewed as dangerous. Killing and surviving had a symbiotic relationship, "You are scared, really scared," and so "you kill because that little SOB is doing his best to kill you, and you desperately want to live, to go home, to get drunk or walk down the street on a date again."[177] Some soldiers were convinced that their primary duty was to kill ("that is what we are here for—to kill gooks"), the tied duty to survival, "Kill gooks and make it home alive. Once they're dead they leave you the hell alone."[178] In the case of survival, the body count became an important tool: The more enemies dead, they believed, the less chance of themselves being killed. Lieutenant Calley noted that even before My Lai the men in his unit called themselves the "Death Dealers." His men would say that they would like to kill every man, woman, and child in South Vietnam. If they were all wiped out, their own survival would be ensured, and they could return home alive: "If I kill everyone, then I can leave." This was the logic that supported their argument. [179] And the belief was not confined to Calley's troops. "If you wanna live, ya gotta kill," a commander used to tell his men, before leading them to the field.[180]

THE MAKING OF HEROES

However, some memoirs of fighting in Vietnam represent killing done with a transport and dedication that completely obscures the desperation, vengeance, and sickness that tormented others. Nor were the soldiers in these memoirs animated solely by the resolve to survive. In the narrative, *We Were Soldiers Once, and Young*, the combatants had no qualms and no indecision about confronting and killing the enemy. It caused these warriors neither a personal crisis nor produced psychotic behavior. The killing was done neatly and in a rare instance of "vicious hand-to-hand" fighting, efficiently. One of these surveyed the field after a battle. The mayhem overwhelmed and pleased him, "My God, there has been a heavy battle here. Hell, there are bodies all over this valley down through here. For the last thirty minutes we have just been walking around and over and through bodies to get here. You guys have been playing combat for real here." Not one emotion or disturbing thought is expressed in the narrative concerning the human cost, nor is there an estimate of the war's cause or aims. The commander thanked the troops for their performance, telling them to be proud of what they did, especially because it was done for their country. An underlying complacency toward violence permeates *We Were Soldiers Once, and Young*. Bravery matters more than the loss of comrades, the futility of war, and even defeat. Looking back on the deeds represented in the narrative, a veteran intones a nostalgic refrain, "Those were the days, my friend." [181] Those days were spent killing and dying with unmatched intensity, made memorable for their individual prowess. Screenwriter John Milius understood the dark pulse of violence when he said, [War] "is unspeakably attractive. People enjoy intensity. The human animal seems to be drawn to it like a moth to a flame." [182] Truly, this excitement and intensity are conveyed in the following scene in *We Were Soldiers Once*. A battalion leader intrepidly leads his troops out of a helicopter and toward the tree line, firing his rifle all the while. No fear or doubt troubled him or his men during what in the Vietnam campaign was generally recognized as the most dangerous of all actions, the helicopter combat assault in a hot landing zone. One platoon went right away "in hot pursuit" of fleeing enemy soldiers; another opened fire, causing the enemy to break both left and right; another group of soldiers charged past the trees while firing their M-16 on full automatic; one combatant "pumped grenade after grenade into the screaming Vietnamese." The momentum of the North Vietnamese attack was stopped as the Americans "stood firm" and "mowed them down." Platoon leader Savage "personally killed fifteen to twenty enemies." A sergeant was struck by a bullet above his heart that went out under his left arm. While bleeding heavily, "he grabbed a rifle and fought on." His company "held its ground in a stunning display of personal courage and unit discipline." A sergeant paid his respects to two of his fallen soldiers found slumped across their silent M-60 machine gun, surrounded by piles of empty shell casings and ammunition cans. It is exciting news: "Courageous machine gunners inflicted heavy casualties on a large North Vietnamese reinforcement." They "did a great job. They kept firing that gun and didn't leave it. They stayed on it to the end," fighting with skill and zest. [183] Death and suffering are overlooked in favor of the fighting. The combatants of *We Were Soldiers Once, and Young* ignored the human cost of the battle and its power to traumatize the men. They did not recoil at the loss of their comrades; they were emotionally detached from the human and intellectual consequences of the battle, and in spite of there being no ultimate victory over the Viet Cong, they were not disheartened. They believed they had accomplished something important. "With our sacrifices," the narrators conclude, "we had learned... something important about ourselves. We could stand against the finest light infantry in the world and hold our ground."[184] They had qualified as warriors in the fiercest of struggles. Perhaps they possessed the making of military heroes. But the killing, which occupies center stage throughout the narrative, confers value unselectively on war and warring, and in this case, the value was hard to defend. Apparently, for these soldiers, such abstractions were insignificant compared to their ability to endure and sacrifice. Despite its being a source of self-confidence and pride, their military prowess served no higher purpose. It was an end in itself.

Robin Moore's memoir, *The Green Berets*, registers another example of combatants killing with relish and abandon in which the same spirit and goal that animated the combatants of *We Were Soldiers Once, and Young* is actively expressed. The Green Berets were widely despised. The saying, "If you kill for money, you are a mercenary. If you kill for pleasure, you are a sadist. If you kill for both, you are a Green Beret,"[185] easily explains why, in prowess alone, there is no human excellence. Ferocious fighters, they took unusual pleasure in killing, as the following ambush shows:

"Suddenly heavy automatic rifle and machine-gun fire raked the advancing, black-uniformed men from the rear. The Rangers cheered as the Communists fell, torn and bloody, to the ground. They were catching intense fire from both sides... In front of us, the Communist main positions were shaken by new blasts of 81-mm. mortar rounds... The VC on our flanks withdrew. But the strike-force companies were upon them before they could even start back for their main positions. Demoralized, the Communists, who minutes before thought they were about to destroy us, were trapped between their intended victims and heavily armed companies that had appeared from nowhere. Their only chance of escape was to the south, away from the remainder of their battalion. Turning in that direction, they were raked by fire from B Company." Officer Arklin brought the ambush to a climax: He "picked up a small hand detonator, gave the handle a sharp twist, and there was an ear-splitting explosion along the entire length of the ambush. Screams came from the ditch. Pieces of legs, arms, heads, and unidentifiable red meat blasted onto the road."

The Green Berets and their Vietnamese followers "shrieked with chilling glee at the mayhem wreaked on the hated enemy."[186] No one ever questioned the fierce fighting and ruthless killing done by these exceptional soldiers. They were cold and efficient killers who greatly valued the perfection of their art.

The combatants of *The Green Berets* are different in their mentality and performance under fire than those of the novels and memoirs explored earlier. The Green Berets' memoirs depicted men fully convinced of the worthiness of their actions. They had no second thoughts and no qualms. They believed in the official cause, (that which the majority of writers and memorialists repudiated) fighting Communism and asserting American power on a worldwide stage. Robin Moore closes the narrative, "What the outcome in Vietnam will be is anybody's guess, but whatever happens, Special Forces men will continue to fight Communism and make friends for America in the underdeveloped nations that are the targets of Communist expansion."[187] But, heroism in a war in which soldiers fight with neither ideal nor deeply felt causes, must be considered a vice.

TRAINING

Although endurance and sacrifice are essential ingredients in heroic deeds, they do not come out of nowhere or even naturally to a soldier. The reason the killing fields left the narrators and protagonists of *We Were Soldiers Once... and Young* and *The Green Berets* undaunted before the grim task of dealing out death wholesale had to do with their training. They were well prepared for their work, following, no doubt, the guidelines laid down by military manuals. One of these entitled, *On Killing*, tackles the main problem facing men sent to war—guilt and remorse. The proper training of recruits, it advises, should consist of instilling the "moral direction and philosophical guidance" necessary for killing without any sense of guilt or remorse. Apparently, the combatants of both *The Green Berets* and *We Were Soldiers Once* had absorbed the guidelines laid out in that work. They were able to face "the moral and social burdens" of killing with indifference to violence and suffering. Because of this, the horror and fear of their own death and that of others had no power over them. This simple prescription was set forth by a former Army Ranger and current professor of Military Science at Arkansas State University. In it, the author states that it is not enough to condition soldiers to trust the leadership to make decisions for them. They must be taught to understand the "Weinberger doctrine," that is, in order to be good killers, free from the torments and breakdowns that follow their acts, they need to handle "the moral and social burdens" of their deeds. First, they must be made to see the vital interest of the country, the political and military objectives of the war, and be confident that the war is supported by the people at home. Second, they must be reassured that what they do on the battlefield is morally "right and necessary." Give the soldier a cause, which is deemed to be reasonable, and he will find within himself the fighting spirit necessary to carry on killing without grief or doubt. Moral direction and philosophical guidance can also be provided by commanders, families, and society. These, the author warns, must understand a soldier's desperate need for recognition and acceptance and the need to be constantly reassured that what he will be asked to do is just and necessary. Society, too, must see the killing as virtuous so that it can lend its support. If the military and civilian personnel would grasp the meaning and value of the above doctrines and their consequences, in which case society would be both accomplices and supporters of his action, they could influence the soldier and help him become an efficient killer immune from inner pain.[188]

On Killing sets forth a cause for the soldiers to believe in, the vital interest of the country, and makes clear the political and military objectives of the war. It emphasizes that the cause is not the expression of the individual soldier, but that of the policy that happens to hold sway at the time of any particular war. The warriors of *We Were Soldiers Once. . . and Young* and *The Green Berets* strongly believed in American power and using it against a perceived Communist threat. That was their cause. To have been immersed in killing without suffering the psychic disruptions that beset the soldiers of other narratives and memoirs, these Special Forces most certainly had internalized the philosophical and moral direction imparted by their trainers. They were eager to kill; their killing made them proud and left their consciences unperturbed. But could all soldiers be inoculated with the same belief and cause? Of course not. In Vietnam, there were many combatants who had no use for the moral and philosophical guidance provided by *On Killing*. As many novelists and memorialists have shown, they implicitly rejected the belief that the war was fought for the vital interest of the country and consequently, could not accept the military leadership's prescription for killing without guilt. As a result, they were unable to carry the burden of war, and their souls were crushed under it. No amount of moral or philosophical guidance could neutralize the effects of the mutual barbarization and needless cruelties perpetrated far beyond military necessity. They were rebels, but they were also the unknowing instruments of renewal that could have come from the Vietnam experience. It was Bernard Fall's hope that in the future, combatants and non-combatants alike would turn against the war, and in that, there would be renewal.[189]

THE MAN I KILLED

Already in the midst of the war, some combatants tried to let human compassion prevail over needless cruelties. One of them, author and veteran Larry Heinemann, succeeded in placing the value of life above the demands of war. Heinemann who had lost his comrade and best friend had become one of those maniac soldiers who devoted his time and energy to killing. "You get mean for real. You start volunteering for the weird missions, all the goofy ambushes, loaded to the teeth with grenades and knives, and your cool-ass AK. I dug free-fire zones because we could kill anything that moved, and all I wanted to do was kill and kill and burn and rape and pillage until there was nothing left." However, even as he indulged his killing impulse, he realized that his soul was being destroyed, "The war has swallowed me, it has clamped off all the veins, and I am high on dope and Darvon and mo-gas and sick and tired." He is more than simply sick and tired. "I am filthy all the time. I feel that grit, that crawl of the skin, something itching all the time, and greasy… It is something inside, some white silky liquid, gathering itself around a blackened marrow." Degraded and enslaved by his battlefield life, he was aware that he could never recapture his old self and live a normal life: "I can never go home. . . Nobody goes home from here." Despite the loss, his tension and energy were directed toward recapturing what the war had taken from him. Heinemann would never live as a normal human being again, but in becoming tragically aware of his loss and not giving up on regaining the pure soul he once was, he succeeded in placing life above the demands of war. He clings to it with undying love, "I just want to see it. I won't say a thing... I just want to see it one more time. I want to smell it, touch ever so lightly, put my ear to it and hear it tap, tap, tap."[190]

Often with help from the creative power of the mind thoughts fly from affliction. Such is the manner in which Tim O'Brien countered the overwhelming grief that threatened to destroy his life. He imagined how his victim might have lived, had he not killed him. In one singular instance, unique in its explicit repudiation of killing and the only instance of its kind in Vietnam fiction and non-fiction where the killing of the enemy is no longer justified as military duty, life is sovereign. O'Brien is profoundly grieved after having killed another human being. In "The Man I Killed" he recalls the time he was contemplating the dead soldier lying face-up in the center of a trail. He dreams the dead man to life, imagining the father, the uncles, and the neighbors of the fallen soldier had once fought for independence from the French. "He was not a Communist. He was a citizen and a soldier." He was afraid of war but had accepted the teaching that "to defend the land was a man's highest duty and highest privilege." He fought and died, believing in a noble cause. He "had no stomach for violence. He loved mathematics." O'Brien has created a fully rounded character whose hopes and dreams confront him as a living reality. "The man I killed would have been determined to continue his education in mathematics... He devoted himself to his studies. He spent his nights alone, wrote romantic poems in his journal, took pleasure in the grace and duty of differential equations." O'Brien does not accept the fact that the enemy soldier is dead. The man he killed would forever be a part of his life as a living being, "I'll look up and see the young man coming out of the morning fog. I'll watch him walk toward me, his shoulders slightly stooped, his head cocked to the side. He'll pass within a few yards of me and suddenly smile at some secret thought and then continue up the trail to where it bends back into the fog."[191] Compassion and sorrow led him to resurrect his former enemy with a life enshrined by expectation and potential for happiness. In this way, he was able to preserve and protect his own soul.

III

THE DYING

HIDING THE TRUTH

In the early stages of the war, military strategists reported the "facts" veiled in euphemisms in order to hide its horrors. To maintain public support, they covered up images like that of a South Vietnamese officer shooting a Viet Cong in the head on a street in Saigon, or children burned by napalm, running, and screaming on a road. The cover-up worked for a while, but as the public perceived the cause itself unworthy, its support began to weaken. One veteran of WW II, the literary scholar, and critic, Paul Fussell, made a public career out of refusing to disguise or elevate it. "War, he said, reduced human beings to serial numbers, 'quasi-mechanical interchangeable parts, and their opponents to vermin who could be slaughtered with 'crazy brutality and sadism.'"[192] As a remedy, the strategists then proposed to reveal the truth and show the horrors, the intention being to habituate people to the war's atrocities and make the cold, hard facts acceptable. But when the growing number of fatalities due to ambushes, land mines, and booby traps eventually became known, the revelation had the opposite effect. The war appeared to be the "most destructive, the most horrible, the most terrible" of all the wars ever waged in the history of the world. It shocked the public and weakened its support.[193] As Bernard Fall reflected, "it is in the nature of civilized people to be hurt by the horrors of war and to want to stop them." [194] These reflections are an indirect acknowledgment of the extraordinary ravages that pervaded this war. They matter a great deal as signs of the quantity and quality of American casualties, not simply as facts disturbing the conscience and sensibility of the public, but because the kind of war that General Westmoreland had decided to wage demanded an unusually high number of victims and often appalling deaths.

It is generally acknowledged that young men barely out of adolescence are the risk-takers who have not yet taken to heart the reality of death. Most live under the illusion they are immortal. It was no different for the young recruits in Vietnam. Death was unacceptable. They did not believe in it and were reluctant to confront it either on or off the battlefield. These young "gods" had at their disposal the most advanced military technology and weaponry in the world, aircraft, helicopters, and tanks, against a people whose military means were, by comparison, primitive. Their weapons were programmed to get rid of the enemy promptly and efficiently while keeping the individual soldier at a distance, and it was generally assumed that they would succeed in destroying the enemy. Unfortunately, they were psychologically unprepared for the brutal close-up encounters of primitive warfare.

The battlefield revealed half of the truth of Washington's policy, that the United States could display its awesome power against the enemy. The other half, that its technological superiority failed to crush the enemy, became an affront to the first. Instead of being mere tools to enhance the fighting spirit of the combatants, the tremendous power of their weaponry encouraged men with no deeply held convictions to depend exclusively on their weapons. Only a few believed strongly enough in Washington's policy to embrace a cause that would transcend the suffering and sustain the fighting spirit. Even though the advanced weaponry was frighteningly in evidence, the Americans were unable to defeat the enemy promptly and efficiently. The Viet Cong were surprisingly aggressive and resilient and able to inflict on Americans many more losses than expected while the Americans were daily facing their own deaths without reporting any victory worthy of the loss. Meanwhile, the shocking reality of death took hold of their young minds and imaginations. Dying and killing became a kind of personal affair that surpassed the official goal of displaying and establishing American power. Because the essential foundation—a deeply felt cause—was missing, fear and other emotions took over. The misery of battle, what strategist Summers called "the horrors of war," caused them to feel the futility of the entire war scene. It began to undermine the moral and intellectual values of the combatants and cut down their fighting spirit. "Abusing the land until it became unworkable, killing and being killed, and yet nothing changing," was the way a soldier and impartial observer of the battlefield portrayed the destructive activity of the Americans fighting in Vietnam. [195] It was impossible to find among them soldiers who died believing in a cause such as those that Glenn Gray had known on the battlefields of World War II. Those soldiers sacrificed their lives willingly, out of love either for their country, a glorified leader, or an ideal. Death was a mere happenstance on the way to victory. It proved their love and devotion to something beyond themselves; it was the necessary means to fulfilling a cause. [196] Death and wounds initially appeared to be only remote possibilities for the young recruits in Vietnam. It was tacitly assumed that their superior offensive power would quickly bring the enemy to its knees. But when violence struck them the same as it did all soldiers on the battlefields of past wars, it affected them grievously. Perhaps it was because their expectations were too high, and their knowledge of death was limited by youth and inexperience. Whatever the reason, it is evident from the pens and memoirs of those that lived and suffered in Vietnam that a search for the meaning of death had become an obsession peculiar to this war. There is no doubt that in past wars the fallen have offered a spectacle that distressed and depressed the survivors. But the reports that came out of Vietnam have stirred the imagination and emotions of both soldiers and observers in ways unknown to the witnesses and protagonists of earlier wars. The veterans of this war carry a special taint, a taint that consists of an excess of images and "encounters with the dead and dying."[197]

GHOSTS

Death on the battlefield took center stage. In *Going After Cacciato*, a novel whose realism turns on a surreal element, the failure of soldiers struggling to stay alive in a harsh environment marks them from the very beginning of the narrative. The first paragraph is a threnody: "It was a bad time. Billy Boy Watkins was dead, and so was Frenchie Tucker. Billy Boy had died of fright, scared to death on the field of battle, and Frenchie Tucker had been shot through the nose. Bernie Lynn and Lieutenant Sidney Martin had died in tunnels. Pederson was dead and Rudy Chassler was dead. Buff was dead. Ready Mix was dead. They were all among the dead[198]

Why the emphasis on death instead of courage or the value of sacrifice or the resolve to be victorious? Why is the sense of loss and lament placed at the very beginning of this work? The author lets the reader know that these protagonists, who will appear in the course of the story are ghosts. He announces their demise even before they speak or make a move. They are in fact defined by their deaths. None of them had a cause to show for their sacrifice, and their departure is marked by brief explanations indicating that there was no other way to go but six feet under. The narrative strategy creates from the beginning the perception that the unit, which is supposedly attempting to capture the fugitive Cacciato, has achieved no victories only subjective progressive annihilation. The opening chapters announce the conclusion to the preceding actions, which were nothing more than ceaseless thrashing around that resulted in a number of casualties. Yet, even though the narrative shows that death rules the battlefield, it is also infused with a spirit of life. For those still living, there is an effort to find a way out of the war and to avoid the violence that has cut down their comrades. Cacciato at least had found a way out of the war. Yet, in pursuing him, the reader can never be certain whether his comrades were really trying to bring him back or to follow his example.

As the war approached its inevitable end, the presence of death never left the Americans. It was made even more vivid by the Tet offensive. General Westmoreland tried vainly to present Tet as an American victory, but for the soldiers who fought the enemy on the streets and in buildings, it was a defeat. In its aftermath, a keen observer noted, that all of Vietnam "was a dark room full of deadly objects. The VC were everywhere all at once like spider cancer, and instead of losing the war in little pieces over years, we lost it fast in under a week. After that, we were like the character in pop grunt mythology, dead but too dumb to lie down." [199] Death had the upper hand; the Americans saw no other path but the one that led to more death.

THE PERVASIVENESS OF DEATH

Given its overall presence and the scarce control Americans had over it, death came to be regarded, not as a price that had to be paid for victory, but as a calamity. They detested it and did their best to avoid it. The war managers knew how the combatants felt and took bizarre steps to counteract their perception. Because it was recognized that its graphic presence had a dramatic effect on the observers, some officers inferred that a first-hand knowledge of it would get the soldiers "used to the sight of blood," the assumption being that the sight of blood would entice them to spill it, inure them to it, and get them to overcome their abhorrence. A close acquaintance with the gory reality would harden the recruits and stir up their fighting instinct. On one occasion a colonel ordered that four enemy bodies, which were about to be taken to the cemetery, be kept in a trailer and displayed to the administrative personnel. The bodies stank horribly but that did not deter the colonel's resolve. Such a display was, of course, a ridiculous and grotesque maneuver, and it left the onlookers indifferent at best. One by one the Marines walked up to the trailer, "looked into it… then walked back to their desks and typewriters," probably disgusted, rather than fortified, by the sight of blood. However, that was not the end, because once the dead were finally removed, a captain came back to the lieutenant in charge and ordered him to bring them back to be displayed again, this time for the benefit of General Robert Thompson, the chief advisor to General Westmoreland who was coming for a briefing. The display of the bodies, the colonel presumably believed, would let him understand that his unit was familiar with death and ready to face it. [200]

But it was impossible to prepare the soldiers in advance of the experience. For them, it was the close-up encounters of death in the field that shook them and proved psychologically as well as physically devastating. Safety in Vietnam was non-existent. Violence constantly shadowed the soldiers, even in places thought to be safe: "You could be in the most protected space in Vietnam and still know that your safety was provisional, that early death, blindness, loss of legs, arms or balls, major and lasting disfigurements... would come in on the freaky fluky as easily as in the so-called expected ways." Such unusual deaths and wounds were frequent occurrences. They had eliminated many more Americans from the battlefield than were officially recognized, "You heard so many of those stories it was a wonder anyone was left alive to die in firefights and mortar-rocket attacks." Death's pervasive presence made the soldiers feel like marked men. They could not relax, and neither could they afford to feel comfortable in certain places and at certain times; if they did, they invited the enemy to attack, to "come over and take a giant shit on" them. [201]

THE ENVIRONMENT

In addition to the aggressive and successful tactics of the enemy, another entity enhanced the presence of death. The environment in which they had to live and fight, evoked both in their imagination and in reality, fear bordering on terror. The environment was death's vestibule. The heath was an invulnerable enemy. It pounded on the soldiers' helmets in such a way that they regarded it, not as a condition of weather, but as a "thing malevolent and alive." [202] The jungle was "God's green furnace," and it seemed that "God had made this jungle for the Marines," that He must have had "a hard-on for Marines"—made them his whipping boys "because we kill everything we see." The human enemy was not nearly as threatening. "Our real enemy is the jungle," a veteran pinpointed the source of danger.[203] "Forget the Cong," a reporter came to realize, "the trees would kill you, the elephant grass grew up homicidal, the ground you were walking over possessed malignant intelligence, your whole environment was a bath."[204] The heat bled the color from the faces of the men, it could "kill" a man, and it could "bake his brains, or wring the sweat out of him until he dropped from exhaustion." The soldiers' eyes took on a blank expression known as the "thousand-yard stare." [205] Captain Beaupre, the protagonist of Halberstam's novel, *One Very Hot Day*, was still alive after marching on a Search and Destroy mission, but he was one of the walking dead: he had died "many hot deaths from the sun."[206] In the jungle American courage vanished. Five minutes after entering it, a combatant was fighting for his life. His uniform was heavy with sweat, and he had difficulty breathing. "It was like being locked in a sick room with a vaporizer jammed on high." Clouds of small bugs swarmed about his face, going in and out of his mouth, and some he swallowed. Drops of sweat slid across the lenses of his glasses, and the forest appeared to him as "a swirling blob of shimmering green." His pack grew heavier, the straps cut into his shoulders. His back ached. His feet hurt. Heat "steamed from the soil." In the distorted vision of the soldiers, even the sun was green. They were "being baked" as if in an oven and felt lost with "no way out."[207] They came to believe that both land and sun conspired with the Viet Cong, "wearing us down, driving us mad, killing us." In this war, the enemy could attack without engaging in firefights and escape as soon as it struck. As a result, the Americans felt "more victims than soldiers." [208] They were unable to summon the aggressive will to fight both the VC and the terrain, for the VC and land were one. The men became . . . "wild as hell. You spend a month in the bush, and you are not a Marine anymore. Hell, you are not even a goddamn person."[209] Plodding along in the grip of exhaustion through bush and jungle, they were the "young newly made old" whose bodies carried "their own corpses of youth." [210]

DEATH'S RAVAGES

What happens to human bodies on the battlefield has no theatrical possibilities. The explosion of a mine near a combatant had the effect of mixing "trousers with calf muscles and tendons with genitals with intestines with bladder with shit with livers and spleen and kidneys and stomachs, and it jammed the oozy mass up into lungs and throats." [211] The presence of violence and death was real and powerful enough to produce sickness. "We were sickened by the torn flesh, the viscera, and the splattered brains," a marine recorded his response to the sight of mutilated bodies. [212] The proximity produced a traumatic effect. The recovery of bodies after a skirmish, for instance, forced soldiers to handle them. This made the recovery as harrowing an experience as the battle itself, "The dead were everywhere. Some lay in piles. Some lay alone" in weird postures. "One seemed to kneel. Another was bent from the waist over a small boulder, the top of his head on the ground, his eyes rigid, the eyes squinting in concentration as if he were about to perform a handstand or somersault." If the fallen had been dead for more than one day, they "were all badly bloated. Their clothing was stretched tight like sausage skins, and when we picked them up some made sharp burping sounds as the gases were released. They were heavy. Their feet were bluish green and cold. The smell was terrible." As a result of his contact with the decomposing bodies of his comrades, the narrator of this episode lived "the worst day of the war."[213]

The spectacle of death so violent, consisting of the brutal and repulsive aspects of the fallen, grievously unsettled those who witnessed it. At the end of an artillery attack on the Bravo company, while approaching the Demilitarized Zone, the combatants looked around and connected right away with death. They saw "chunks of flesh and boots. Next, they began to find the dead and wounded, dazed, and moaning in the grass below." "Some had been blown a hundred meters off the hill. All who had stayed to fight... were dead." The survivors' emotions revealed nothing patriotic and nothing about the military value of the operation, "With death and pain all around, the living fell on a variety of roles," none of them befitting proud soldiers. Some "fell back on a religious discipline, some just fell apart and reverted to a dazed and preadolescent disbelief . . . a superficial joy in refuting the obvious... A few held a stoic dignity." The survivors engaged in an interior struggle to find the balance that the spectacle of violence had broken. Immersed in the aura of death, they searched the grass and underbrush for its victims. "That is all I remember that day," one of them recalled, "carrying guys I knew up that hill in a poncho. Up and down, up and down, all day long. I was in a daze all day; I did not know what was happening." Absorbed in his task, he thought the world was death itself, "I started thinking the whole world was like this, and I was doing normal things."²¹⁴ The stench conspired to sink the combatant into that world by penetrating deeply into his being, both material and immaterial. The stench was "unique" and probably the most offensive on earth; it had a devastating effect on soldiers, as devastating as the sight of death. Once a soldier has smelled it, he "can never again believe with conviction that man is the highest being in earthly creation." The stench was intrusive and caused in some combatants an inner deterioration, the feeling of belonging to a race of men different than the one he had always lived with.²¹⁵

The body was supreme in all its aspects. Pain and death were a leveler that knew neither friend nor foe when it came to exhibiting its raw ugliness. The enemy dead were equally degraded, thus denying the Americans any real sense of victory or superiority. The enormous number of enemy dead was graphically represented. "The collage of death poses, the pale gray skin, the curled fingers scraping the grass ash and filmy dirt—represented in a variety of poses, some sticking their tongues out of bloody black mouths, one dink with his head sheared off at the jaw with his black tongue laid out on his lowers, looking for all the world like somebody took his head off with a swipe of a hand, one dude with eyes tight, lips open, the wrinkled laugh lines and frown lines, and black blood down to here from the mass of dry shredded junk hanging from the chest—the dink caught a claymore fair and square. And the dudes behind him hanging on to one another. The dead leading the dead, all in line, and all laid out." These descriptions bordered on a kind of sensual fascination that had little to do with the success of American tactics or victory.²¹⁶ In past wars, the enemy's dead would ordinarily be related to the skill and valor of the victors, but in this one, it made no difference whether the death was that of a friend or foe; death was universally horrific. The slaughtered enemy might have symbolized American bravery and made the soldiers proud. But the bodies were represented as repulsive objects, not as trophies of American prowess. Their ghastly appearance merely served to remind the young men of death's constant and overwhelming presence and to intensify the expectation of their own death and dismemberment. They loathed and feared it.

FEAR

Fear alone could kill. A veteran imaginatively remembers the passing away of a comrade who had "died of fright, scared to death, on the field of battle."[217] Generally, however, the fear created a need to control it; pride and conditioning made soldiers reluctant to show it. Fear and the eagerness to conceal it forced them to lie to themselves. Some did it by staring death in the face and putting up a psychological defense, pretending that it "was not the terrible thing it was." This was useful if one could believe in one's own argument. Then one could respond with a shrug, a grin, resignation, or indifference. Other combatants resigned themselves to go quickly and quietly rather than living in fear, or worse, complaining or resisting its hold on them. "They were afraid of dying but they were even more afraid to show it." Showing it was regarded as weakness, and pride helped many to control it. "Men killed and died because they were embarrassed not to." To preserve their dignity many chose death "so as not to die of embarrassment." The survivors tried to reduce these deaths to ordinary events since they expected them to happen to them as well.[218] But for others, simple resignation was impossible. They wanted to rid themselves of the entire vision of death. At the end of a narrative dealing with helicopter pilots, one of them who was a short-timer with one month left to his tour wanted to stop flying to avoid injury or death in order to make sure he would return home. However, there had to be a medical reason for exemption from flying. Fear qualified. The doctor was willing to grant the exemption and ground the pilot, provided he admitted he was too afraid to fly. But no such admission was forthcoming, since the pilot felt that by making it, he would confess cowardice. Being too proud, he kept on flying, resigned to the wishes of his commanding officers. He suffered from insomnia, took sedatives to function, lost weight, was worn out, and looked "like shit." He wanted to go home but not enough to admit his fear of flying and be branded a coward. He kept on flying his helicopter, which became a suicidal activity in the hopes that death, perhaps, would cut short the misery of his soldiering life.[219]

Suicide was deliberately sought when it looked like a true release from the terror of the battlefield. On a Search and Destroy operation towards the end of his tour, Lieutenant Caputo and his platoon loaded with gear were marching through an area where they expected to hit at least one mine or be ambushed. He felt that the probability of death was high, but despite the more than forty pounds of equipment he was carrying, he felt "a wonderful, soaring lightness." The reason for this feeling was "a sudden and mysterious recovery from the virus of fear." He had ceased "to be afraid of dying," not because he was seized by the beauty of the sacrifice he would make, but because the knowledge that he was going to die was for him a way out of his nightmare. The persuasion that he had become unworthy of life supported his choice: "I would die as casually as a beetle is crushed under a boot heel, and perhaps it was the recognition of my insect-like pettiness that had made me stop caring. I was a beetle." (His degradation did not, however, prevent him from calling the embrace of death "sublime" and "liberating.") He then cared only about having a quick and painless death. This enabled him to face it with joy. When he and his troops came under artillery fire and death moved toward him, he had an out-of-body experience. He described his inner state: "I felt an ineffable calm, I could see the flashing shells, but they no longer frightened me, because I was a spirit. I saw myself lying face down in the foxhole... I felt no fear, just a great calm and a genial contempt for the puny creature cringing in the foxhole below me." He wondered if he were dying and discovered that "dying was actually pleasant. It was painless," a sweet pleasure after pain. Death had become a powerful narcotic, a cure-all, the "ultimate anesthetic."[220] The painlessness is, of course, a myth, but death served to eliminate fear once and for all, and for that reason, it became a worthwhile goal. A popular song and a favorite one of the Marines echoed the feelings of Lieutenant Caputo in welcoming the end as the beginning of a peace that knows no anxiety:

> I am not scared of dyin'
> And I don't really care
> If it's peace you find in dyin'
> Well then let my time be near
> If it's peace you find in dyin'.[221]

Some soldiers endowed with a tougher temper believed they could overcome fear and despair by imagining themselves invulnerable to the thought and touch of death. They personified it, and like the ancient heroes of darkness, challenged Death as an enemy they would defeat. A derisive variation of the biblical Psalm 23 on the jackets of some soldiers read: "Yea, though I walk through the Valley in the Shadow of Death, I shall fear no Evil, because I am the meanest motherfucker in the Valley."[222] The soldier presumes to fight evil with evil. He can defy the adversary, Death, only when he thinks of himself as more powerful than it. Only a few were able to respond with such defiance, though. Most succumbed to a sense of doom. Death appeared to operate according to an inexorable law, "We live by the law of the jungle," one combatant recalls, "which is that more Marines go in than come out." [223] Who these would be no one could tell, of course, but the law of the jungle ensured that many would die, and they carried the emotional baggage of men on the edge of an abyss: "Grief, terror, love, longing."[224] The sense of doom increased their isolation, for unaided by some theory or training, they had to respond to the ordeal of the battlefield alone and in their own, personal way. In any case, no training could get a soldier accustomed to living in an environment so saturated by the continual demise of friends and comrades. Killing techniques can be taught, but no technique for coping with interior suffering can be fully conveyed; he who comes face to face with death is entirely on his own. In the field, the combatants discovered aspects of war completely unknown to them in civilian life and learned things that could not be taught in a training camp, "What fear feels like and what death looks like, and the smell of it, the experience of killing, of enduring pain and inflicting it, the loss of friends and the sight of wounds."[225] Disabled by fear, the soldiers knew that while serving time in Vietnam they were bound to be ruled by the horrors of the war.

FATALISM

Because violence struck often and in a variety of ways, the combatants knew that sooner or later they would be victims of what seemed to them an unforgiving fate. In Khe Sanh, an outpost frequently bombarded and attacked by the enemy, an American soldier learned more about the variety of wounds he would be exposed to than about ways to defend against the enemy. There could be head wounds, chest wounds, stomach wounds, and "the wound of wounds," the loss of the sexual organs. Then there were the multi-forms of death: "You could die in a sudden blood-burning crunch as your chopper hit the ground like dead weight, you could fly apart so that your pieces could never be gathered, you could take one neat round in your lung and go out hearing only the bubble of the last few breaths, you could die in the last stage of malaria with that faint tapping in your ears… You could be shot, mined, grenaded, rocketed, mortared, sniped at, blown up and away so that your leavings had to be dropped into a sagging poncho and carried to Graves Registration."[226] The forms that death could take made it nearly impossible for the combatants to cling to a cause, if they had one, or to find one as a justification or acceptance of death; they knew that it was very hard to stay out of its range. Any of the types of wounds that his comrades suffered might eventually be his own. In this near certainty, belief in a cause was unthinkable. Death was the world they inhabited day after day, and it did not take a great deal of imagination to see that they could be its victim at any time. Under such conditions making a sacrifice for the victory of their unit or their country became irrelevant.

The enemy's offensive tactics gave American soldiers another reason to consider themselves doomed. The enemy was usually invisible. It frequently ambushed patrols and larger contingents, and it did a great deal of killing by means of land mines and booby traps. The strategy was insidious and effective, and American vulnerability deepened their sense of impending doom. "We could not fight back against the mines or take cover from them or anticipate when they would go off," a veteran recalled. "Walking down the trails, waiting for those things to explode, we had begun to feel more like victims than soldiers."[227] They were often ambushed. When this happened, it was an experience more disquieting even than the spectacle of the dead and the macabre fantasizing that came from that. Taken by surprise, the combatant had the acute sensation that his demise was at hand; he felt death's sting sharp and near. Far from inducing endurance and courage, he was seized by strange helplessness, "You writhe like a man suddenly waking in the middle of a heart transplant," a veteran vividly recorded, "the old heart out, the new one poised somewhere unseen in the enemy's hands. The pain, even with the ether or sodium chloride, explodes in the empty cavity, and the terror is in waiting for the cavity to be filled, for life to start pumping and throbbing again. You whimper, low and screeching, and it does not start anywhere."[228] Other combatants under fire had a more realistic sensation of dying, "I stretch out on my back where I fall," one of them recalled, "breathing open-mouthed, forcing down long, deep drafts. My arms shake, my fingers open and lose just to feel the muscles work against the earth. I am soaked to the skin and fiery hot. There is something jammed in my throat. I feel as though I will have to puke or choke on it. My whole body shudders against loose dirt. My stomach rattles my breathing into short, terrified gasps."[229] Under fire, physical and mental pain converge in the interlacing of mind and body. In some soldiers it created the sensation that they had "already died more than once, squirming under the bullets, going through the act of death and coming through embarrassingly alive. The bullets stop... You tentatively peek up, wondering if it is the end. Then you look at the other men, reading your own caved-in belly deep in their eyes. The fright dies the same way Novocain wears off in the dentist's chair. You promise, almost moving your lips, to do better next time; that by itself is a kind of courage."[230] But there may be no chance of that, for terror alone "would take you out of your head and your body too," a keen observer of the Vietnamese battlefield discovered, leaving the victim incapable of further action.[231]

COMBAT ASSAULT

A tactic widely utilized was called "Combat Assault." It was carried out by helicopters, and the American command regarded it to be a potent offensive tool. But in fact, it often yielded results far below what was expected. Most combatants knew the tactic was faulty as well as the price to pay for its failure. It exposed them to the enemy's fire, causing them to feel defenseless and certain to die or be wounded. Headquarters' insistence on using it rather than a more prudent and cautious option, was perhaps the main reason for creating among the troops a sense of doom. In a combat assault, a soldier recalled, "the thing you think about on the way down is how perfectly exposed you are. Nowhere to hide your head. You are in a fragile machine. No foxholes, no rocks, no gullies."[232] It was a flight to perdition. An assault on a hot landing zone, in particular, assured the soldiers of almost certain death. They jumped out of the helicopters, and the only thing they knew was the enemy shooting, mortars coming in, and people dying and screaming. The attackers were in a singular state: "It is the enclosed space, the noise, the speed, and above all the sense of total helplessness." On the ground, an infantryman can move the best he sees fit for his protection so that at least he has the illusion of defending himself. But in a helicopter under fire "he hasn't even that illusion. Confronted by the indifferent forces of gravity, ballistics, and machinery, he was pulled in several directions at once... Claustrophobia plagued him in that small place: the sense of being trapped and powerless in a machine was unbearable, and yet he had to bear it."[233] He simply had no choice. He could do nothing to change being inside a helicopter taking him into the line of fire. Paralysis set in, and his martial spirit evaporated. But even for those who were excited by this mission and eager to fight on the ground, the result of the assault more often failed because of their exposure to the enemy. One helicopter pilot taking a group to the landing zone, described the soldiers, as "growling and yelling," psyched for battle. They apparently had overcome the feeling of claustrophobia and powerlessness. But as soon as they stepped out and rushed for the tree line, all were immediately dropped by enemy fire.[234] Although they were able to shake the paralyzing fear for a few moments, they fell as easily as others who shuddered in anticipation of their fate. Another reason why a sense of futility was strongly felt in these combat assaults was the suspicion among combatants that the real purpose was to expose them to the enemy, to draw its fire and reveal its location. If true, this was a costly tactic, one that ensured that the attacking soldiers would suffer many casualties: "That was the strategy... letting the enemy have the initiative and strike only when the enemy wanted to strike and how he wanted to strike." Simply to expose the enemy's position, Americans were stripped of protection and exposed to almost certain death, and then, if still alive, to fight. The tactic demanded American deaths even before combat began. "We had to be ambushed first before we could find the enemy."[235] The enemy always had the initiative. The tactic was irrational. It seemed designed, not to prevail, but to yield American deaths, and since it led to failure time and again, it was another disincentive for the combatants to hold to a cause. They could not believe that such a self-defeating tactic would lead to victory. However, in spite of its cost and lack of success, the combat assault by helicopter was never discarded. The helicopter was a distinctive weapon of American power, but for the soldiers who were disgorged on a landing zone, it was the instrument of their doom.

The perception that death constantly hovered over them and that they were fated to die is one reason why most narratives of this war have paid more attention to the human losses than to the success or failure of the military actions. The writers knew the men were doomed by these actions, and the enormous casualties were the conspicuous result that denied their military value. These writers were deeply moved by the souls of the men afflicted by the immediate apprehension of pain and death, for without a cause to cling to, all thoughts were chained to the anticipation of their demise. For this reason, deeds of heroism and thoughts of victory found no place in their reports. One helicopter pilot fulfilling his duty in the battle of Ia Drang Valley survived, and given the extreme danger he had faced, might have considered himself a courageous combatant and a champion of the American cause. Yet, he was unable to feel good about his deeds. He had an eye for the dead too sharp for his own good, and he was overwhelmed by the number and ugliness of the casualties. Having flown the wounded and dead from the battlefield to the hospital, he counted the bodies that had been deposited there earlier and was unable to accept the fact that so many Americans had died, "I couldn't believe how many bodies were piling up outside the tent." He saw them, not as soldiers who had made the supreme sacrifice for their country, but as victims of an unjust fate. The sight elicited no pride in, or admiration for, their past action in battle; they mattered only as an impressive and depressing show of death. The pilot became frightened, "I looked at the pile of dead and shivered." The bodies told him that death had claimed far more lives than could be conceived as simply the inevitable cost of war. The battles produced nothing but dead bodies, and no military successes; it was a victory for Death. As the battle in the Ia Drang Valley unfolded, the pilot's contact with the dead grew closer and more disquieting. He was mystified by the presence of so many fallen, "We had never carried so many dead before. We were supposed to be winning. The NVA were trapped and being pulverized, but the pile of dead beside the hospital tent was growing." Back at camp, he felt "jittery after seeing too much death," a malaise that worsened when he noticed that the recovered bodies were placed in one pile and the loose parts in another. But the definitive shock came when he witnessed the spectacle of death in action. A load of men stepping out of his helicopter could not even reach the tree line and a measure of protection. "They dropped all around us, dying and dead." The expectation that bullets would be coming through the Plexiglas and his bones, "never stopping," seized him. He was petrified by the sight. He snapped out of his trance only when a comrade urged him to move on. Flying from the battlefield to the hospital with another batch of casualties, the thing that impressed him most was the blood draining on the deck of the helicopter, filling the interior with the smell of death, which "seeped out of the zippered pouches and made the living retch." He flew fast to get rid of the smell, but the smell could not be blown away. In the meantime, the newly dead kept piling up at the collection spot where he noticed their "bellies blown open." He sought some comfort in the idea that by going to Pleiku on his first day off 'to drink his brains out,' he would find some relief from the endless sight of death and pain.[236]

But alcohol could not erase the imprint of the sight of those battlefield casualties, for the pilot had to continue flying. In a competitive vein, his commanding officer told his outfit that other companies had suffered more dead than his, implying it seemed, that the frequency of death among helicopter pilots, was a badge of honor and that more should die in solidarity with their fallen comrades and in recognition of the fate awaiting them. "It's our turn now," they realized, as they fell in step with the commander's exhortation to risk the end stoically, "C'mon, you guys, let's get out there and die!" they proclaimed with black humor. The pilot's busing service in the combat zone increased his fear and strained his endurance. In his mind, the fate of the dead he transported became his own. "Scared out of our minds," was how he defined his own and his comrades' inner state. He was living the life of a man sentenced to death; he was "on death row" near the end of his wait.[237]

SEARCH AND DESTROY

Headquarters also used another tactic to send troops in search of enemy sites. It was called Search and Destroy. To carry out this mission the soldiers wandered blind and unprotected through the jungle and rice paddies; the tactic was disparagingly defined "rattle-assing around the country."[238] In theory, finding the enemy and eliminating his military installations—bunkers, tunnels, rice, ammunitions caches, and sanctuaries—was a legitimate goal, but in practice, it usually failed. In this "war of attrition," the commanders believed there was no alternative. General Westmoreland ignored the problems with Search and Destroy, saying blandly that it "was nothing more than an operational term for a tactic." He never understood or pretended not to understand, that the tactic was useless, since it caused many casualties and yielded little success. On the few occasions when they did succeed, the Viet Cong were able to escape through the "sieve-like" American encirclement. But for lack of men, the Americans could not hold the occupied territory permanently, with the result that the land again became a sanctuary and base of operations for the enemy.[239] In one large search and destroy operation (Checkerboard), fifteen thousand American troops beating the bushes failed "to even find the enemy... much less destroy it."²⁴⁰ The villages and territories that had been occupied in the course of the operation were abandoned soon after it ended. In the course of another search and destroy operation on a scale smaller than Checkerboard, the Americans managed to gain control of a large village. They turned it over to the ARVN, and in no time, the North Vietnamese troops and the Viet Cong were back in the village.²⁴¹

In these operations, the Americans were destined either to lose their life or to see the fruits of their effort wasted. As already noted, the enemy was hard to find, yet it was easy for the enemy to find them. They were often ambushed in the midst of an operation and usually suffered heavy losses, as the Viet Cong enjoyed the advantage of surprise. A veteran observer on the battlefield recognized that the main feature of Search and Destroy was the useless sacrifice of American lives, "We send men out on an operation, they kill a few VC, or the VC kill them and then pull out and the VC come right back in. So, we are back where we started." ²⁴² Repeated failures revealed to the combatants that many would be killed or wounded, labeling them fodder for slaughter, rather than victorious in the endeavor. It was impossible for them to believe they were fighting for a worthwhile cause while being deliberately put in harm's way with no hope of conquering and holding territory. They were in fact being used as pawns in a fatal and futile game rather than in a tactic designed for victory.

Given the drawbacks of Search and Destroy and the insistence on using it, the combatants were resigned to a substantial number of casualties. They knew they were fighting to satisfy the egos of those strategists and commanders who had devised the tactic. "The very idea of the search-and-destroy operation is one of enormous logical fallacy," a corpsman noted, pointing to the incredibly absurd assumption underlying it: "You send a patrol out in order to get it ambushed," meaning that "you have to get ambushed before you find the enemy."²⁴³ The ambush became essential to the American tactic. It was a recipe for death and the soldiers' worst experience. It was, remarked a corporal who had more strength than his comrades and picked up those who fell down exhausted on the trail, "a hell of a way for a young guy to spend the best years of his life." ²⁴⁴ The absence of defined battle lines aided the enemy and harmed Americans, so much so that Westmoreland ascribed the high number of casualties among American officers in Vietnam to a front line, which "was nowhere and everywhere."[245] This haze gave the enemy the advantage. "They were nowhere. They were everywhere... It seemed impossible. They were everywhere. It was beginning to make less and less sense. You just wander around trying to kill them until they kill you," the combatant Goodrich mused and asked himself: "Where the hell is the sense in that? It's insane."[246] Getting killed that way was insane, and it was something worse. Like premeditated murder, it was preordained by the strategy, and the combatants knew it.

Regardless of the drawbacks, the Search and Destroy tactic stayed in place. Headquarters felt that the inevitable loss of life had military value. One Colonel Nickerson in his memoir of the war was worried about the excessive number of casualties sustained by a company in his unit. He could not sleep from worrying. During a week-long operation, he lost forty men, mainly to booby traps and mines, and on top of that, he was unable to dislodge the Viet Cong from the position they were holding. Nevertheless, two days later another patrol was sent out, and it was ambushed. Fifteen out of a platoon of thirty-five Marines lost their lives, and the enemy got away. After that, the colonel's perspective changed. To alleviate his anxiety, he declared that the losses did not matter. "Hell, fifteen casualties ain't nothing," he proclaimed. There were three thousand men in this regiment and, he could afford excessive losses. His experience in World War II supported his reasoning, "When I landed at Guadalcanal ninety percent of my platoon was wiped out in an hour," he recalled, and "there were only five or six of us left, but we kept fighting." Thus, he deflected the objection of a lieutenant who argued that if the same tactic continued to be used, within a few weeks a whole company would be lost. But the colonel stuck to his unit's exploit at Guadalcanal, yelling: "We kept fighting, goddamnit!"[247]

Whereas the landing on Guadalcanal had made human losses unavoidable, in Vietnam there were alternatives. Whether or not a different strategy might have reduced the losses, was never on the table since the underlying belief in the nobility of human sacrifice governed the moves on the battlefield. Understandably, the combatants' resentment festered. A major in the American division ordered a Huey helicopter with eleven men on board to land unprotected by the Cobras "to assault a battalion!" One of the soldiers aboard, knowing the fate he was condemned to, responded harshly, "If I get the opportunity," he wrote home to a friend, "I will kill that son-of-a-bitch. I have more hatred and contempt for him than I ever thought I could possibly feel for any human being. If there is one thing I can't abide, it's an armchair leader who sends his men off to die on hopeless, meaningless operations. To be killed is one thing, to die senselessly another."[248]

SACRIFICE

The principle that sacrifice is intrinsically valuable regardless of the goal achieved or lost supported other tactics and directives that condemned the combatants to die or be wounded. Decisions were made that ignored the real forces at play on the battlefield. For example, the commander regarded the situation at Khe Sanh, an outpost which had been under siege for months, with "great optimism." It was an optimism based on falsehoods that came to be known as "smiling in the shambles," pretending to be winning while losing. This optimism held sway not only at Khe Sanh; it was widespread. When casualties were heavy among the Marines, headquarters reported them as light. Defeats and ambushes were turned into temporary tactical moves, and bad weather, which hampered operations and called for halting them, was described as good and even excellent. At Khe Sanh, where "smiling in the shambles" held a prominent place, some commanders made patently absurd statements. When, on the forty-fifth night of shelling by the enemy, General Tompkins, was asked in a press interview about the possibility that the enemy might simultaneously attack the outpost and the nearby bases that the Marines had set up to support the beleaguered city, he replied that that was "exactly" what he and his men wanted the enemy to do! It was an extravagant and untrue statement, for Khe Sanh evinced only a token American force at "the Western Anchor of our Defense," and there was a "shocking" lack of men and weapons against the enemy's artillery. It was well known that, had the attack come, it would have been a disaster. One couldn't help but see the underside of that statement—that headquarters considered the men expendable. In fact, Khe Sanh was eventually abandoned by the Americans. Undismayed, General Westmoreland gave "smiling in the shambles" a new twist. He termed the withdrawal "a Dien Bien Phu in reverse."[249]

Once the soldiers realized that they were being sent to their death with little or no hope of victory, many became desperate. In *Fields of Fire*, one lieutenant, feeling depressed because of another unsuccessful and costly search and destroy operation, was seized by murderous anger. Convinced that he and his men were doomed, he raged internally while thinking of his comrades' fate: "Kill everything ... we are a floating islet waiting to be killed just because those Bastards think we should be killed so that they can have more bodies on their tote boards when the Reacts pulls us out from where we never should have had to go. Those bastards sit somewhere with air conditioners around and Coca-Cola inside them while we drink this goddamn wormy water. We are closer to being gooks than we are to being them, and yet here we are wanting to kill gooks because of this ulcerous anger that eats the insides of my guts."[250] The grim logic of the coming mission's uselessness could only mean that headquarters valued the dead more than the living. The combatants were aware of the mockery of their sacrifice. A veteran recalled his own sense of hopelessness in the execution of this strategy, "We send men out on an operation, they kill a few VC, or the VC kill them, and then pull out and the VC come right back in. So, we are back where we started... I think these boys are getting killed for nothing."[251] Among the survivors, there was rage and regret because the soldiers risked their lives with nothing to show for it.

On the European battlefields of World War II, the presence of death caused nothing like the turmoil and distress it generated among the soldiers in Vietnam. In World War II the soldiers accepted the risk. Perhaps, having been reconciled to its possibility, they could even promote a love for it.[252] In Vietnam, it was considered a meaningless waste of life, and no amount of courage shown in battle could improve the survivors' estimate of their comrades' death. It had been willed, they believed, by their commanders and had no bearing on any achievable goal useful to the unit or the enterprise. Sacrifice did not ennoble the man. Even those who believed in their mission and who stoically did their duty conceded the pointlessness of so many losses. The combatants of *We Were Soldiers Once ... and Young* recalled with pride that on the battlefield they were able to "stand up to" the best infantry in the world. Yet, they implicitly acknowledged that their sacrifices in the Ia Drang battle, for example, yielded no strategic gains and no victory for their country.[253] Despite the heroics, they knew the score. All was in vain.

COURAGE

In 1969 Lieutenant Broyles was reluctant to embrace a cause. Because of his education, and connections, he had expected to serve out his term translating documents in Washington, D.C. Instead, he was sent to Vietnam to command an infantry platoon. He was afraid of dying and could not set aside his fear. In the Los Angeles airport on his way to Vietnam, he took several steps toward desertion. But in the end, he continued his journey, having persuaded himself that the possibility of dying was remote. His decision was reinforced by the sight of the famed island of Iwo Jima from the airplane. It led him to think about the sacrifice made by the Marines twenty-five years earlier, and the thought of that historic battle inspired him to face combat and the possibility of death. "It was not the result, but the courage, that mattered," he decided. The Marines fought and died faithful to their code. For them, courage was their motto. "If you were a real Marine, you did not care that you had it the roughest, that you always got the short end of the stick, that you might fight and die for a fuck-up."[254] They died for a purpose which was, and still is part of the Marine mystique. From the point of view of the unit or the country for which they fought, their death might have no visible purpose. What counted was individual courage.

But adherence to an established code to prove one's courage satisfies a personal end, and though it may at times lead to a military victory, it is divorced from the ideal of fighting for a higher cause or the unit and the country. Often courage may reflect a wish for death. "Our soldiers are brave," Tolstoy wrote in 1855 in a memorandum compiled while serving in Sevastopol, "because death for them is a blessing." [255] Courage is at the core of the Marine philosophy. Their pride is embodied in their code. In Vietnam, it initiated a willingness to fight and to "die for a fuck up" because all that mattered was to follow the code of the Corps. It may have been just bravado, for the individual Marine loathed death and suffered like any other soldier when facing the enemy. Still, they never gave up the belief in their superiority even when their pride led to wasteful deaths. Their penchant to fight recklessly caused them to suffer an elevated number of casualties and the Corps came to be known as the "finest instrument ever devised for the killing of young Americans." Entire squads were wiped out, but the steep losses failed to induce caution. Instead, when they found the mutilated bodies of their comrades, they became enraged and exposed themselves to death by acting on their own and going on "vengeance patrols." Some companies had seventy-five percent casualties. Sometimes in the frenzy of an attack, Marines ambushed other Marines, and at other times they were killed by friendly fire from planes and artillery. They knew "the madness, the bitterness, the horror and doom of it," yet in the style of the Corps, they were enthralled by the horror and heedless of the waste: "They were hip to it, and more: they savored it." They had a perverse sense of life and death. This could be seen for example when they turned a grieving letter to the mother of a fallen comrade into a mockery, "Tough shit, tough shit, your kid got greased, but what the fuck, he was just a grunt."[256] Their way of life was insane, but under the circumstances, predictable. Cockiness made no heroes out of these soldiers, for the Marines like American weaponry were a symbol of power on the battlefield for which its triumphant display was both end and cause. But such causes rarely win battles, and in Vietnam it failed to secure any victory over the enemy.

DUE CAUSE

The vanity of death in this war can be gathered from the observations of an American soldier who, when he returned to Vietnam after the war, had extensive contact with the former enemy. He discovered that the North Vietnamese were moved by a cause to which they were deeply committed, enough to willingly sacrifice life. He discovered that they had an entirely different vision of death, one that made them think and act for reasons contrary to what motivated their American opponents. The Viet Cong regarded death as a necessary risk, if not the means to the realization of their cause. Although they were pounded relentlessly by superior weaponry—helicopters, light and heavy bombers, tanks, and napalm—they overcame suffering and fear with a fighting spirit that finally carried them to victory. They fought and died, not for a show of courage or pride in a military code, but a deeply held belief in the righteousness of their cause—the independence of their country from foreign domination. Those simple common workers and ordinary soldiers became titans. Supported by a due cause and convinced that their sacrifice was useful, the North Vietnamese defied death and turned it into a mark of valor. It enabled them to ride "on the wind of history"[257] They kept streaming down the trail from the North "prepared to die," willing to go on indefinitely to kill and be killed. Their families were resigned to losing their kin and mourning. "We were brave," the American veteran writes about himself and his comrades, but "not brave enough" to prevail. "We were afraid of death, and the Communists were not."[258]

Years later, Henry Kissinger came to the same conclusion, admitting that militarily the Americans were stronger, but in the end, they lost because the Vietnamese were prepared to die for their country and to keep on fighting until they reached their goal, something that Americans were not prepared to do.[259] Threatened by torture and death, a young North Vietnamese officer captured by the Americans told Colonel Hackworth, "I expect to die anyway, fighting for my cause, the freedom of my country Vietnam." [260] Where there was hope for a better future, his willingness to die was tinged with enthusiasm. This willingness was evident in one of their tactics, engaging Americans up close. The Americans might be clearly technological, "not based on individual bravery or superiority of soldier against soldier."[261] The Viet Cong tried to nullify or neutralize the technological superiority of the Americans by engaging them at close range, often as short as thirty meters. This prevented the Americans from using their air and artillery power because if they did, they were likely to hit their own people. The tactic naturally produced Viet Cong casualties higher than usual, since they had to expose themselves to an American small arms fire. But their willingness to risk all proved that death was contingent on obtaining their goal and central to their success. It is worth noting that the North Vietnamese had plenty of historical precedent on their side. They had fought off Chinese incursions and invasions onto their land for centuries. They had seen off the French following a lengthy colonial occupation. At the end of World War II, they had reason to expect support from the western nations for their legitimate claims for independence. To their chagrin, the United States represented the greatest challenge to such claims. Knowing their cause was just, however, gave them tremendous courage. As a result, "tiny men, no bigger than boys," were able to drive out of their country "a race of giants."[262] Ultimately, the Americans were undermined by their own lack of conviction, the exhaustion of war, a hostile natural environment, and dissident, democratic forces on the home front demanding withdrawal. In the final analysis, no due cause was apparent in the fact that claims of "progress" and "body counts" from generals and politicians were greeted with derision in the ranks.

PROVING ONE'S MANHOOD

In spite of this, however, there were Americans who believed that the expression of certain qualities—discipline, pride, and the resolve to act like a real man—made death meaningful and useful. Lieutenant Sidney Martin, a platoon leader in *Going After Cacciato,* with extensive experience in the field, was convinced that the prerequisite for being a successful combatant in Vietnam was the acceptance of death. This, he argued, brings discipline, pride, and self-respect, which in civilian life a man should be ready to show, but rarely has the opportunity. In war, however, he has many opportunities to demonstrate these qualities, for only then does he have the chance to repeatedly confront death. A soldier's duty, then, is to make use of "his full capacities of courage and endurance," a noble undertaking that may very well lead to the loss of life. Martin's view paralleled that of a chaplain who, in another work by O'Brian, made the case for war in exactly the same terms—an occasion for bringing out the best in man. In that work the narrator, O'Brian, feeling depressed, went to see the chaplain to seek help in overcoming his doubts about the rights and wrongs of war. The chaplain told him that war is good because it gives every fighting man a chance to show his inner strength. War may be questioned but not rejected, the chaplain argued, because it raises man above anonymity and gives him the opportunity to show his virtues. "Where the hell do you fit the guts and bravery into your intellectual scheme?" the chaplain demanded, turning war into a golden opportunity for anyone to prove himself a real man.[263] Lieutenant Martin's view on war and virtue takes the chaplain's argument a step further. War may give a man the opportunity to show his mettle, but real virtue depends not only on courage and endurance but also on a soldier's willingness to die, that is, to accept death's possible victory in battle. War is valued, Martin believed, because only in war is man given the chance to confront a violent and early death in the calm assurance of proving his "manhood."[264] In his willingness to die, an otherwise ordinary man has the chance to make himself relevant. Neither purpose nor cause should matter, he states. He could not imagine a soldier dying for a cause, let alone in the collective loyalty to his comrades. The adversary is death itself, and war gives man the "chance to confront death many times," and to show discipline, pride, and self-respect in battle. In Martin's mind, virtue in war is seen in the context of an individual, private morality, not in the wider sense of the war and a cause. Death exists regardless of any cause and leads to no victory but its own. Like the Marine code, his view is an incitement to extravagant risk-taking without any reference to a military goal or objective. In support of his view, he imagined one of his men to be the perfect candidate for realizing this idea of virtue and death on the battlefield, one Private Berlin who was dutiful, energetic, and displayed fortitude, loyalty, self-control, and courage. But he was mistaken, for Berlin had no desire to confront death on the battlefield; he aimed to live a long life. Lieutenant Martin had gained among the men of his platoon a reputation as a worshipper of Death. None thought he was a shining example of military virtue, and no one remembered him for his humanity. He found Death while searching for it in underground tunnels. He was not mourned by his men, rather it was an occasion for reaffirming life. He was replaced by Lieutenant Corson, a leader who earned their loyalty and love. They had good reason to love him: he "took no chances, he wasted no lives. The war... scared him."[265]

Once the American soldiers perceived the vanity of death in war, it was inevitable that it would be seen as the worst thing that could possibly happen to them, "This whole war," a soldier explained on the day before he committed suicide, is "meat," meat "for the bugs."[266] Some soldiers seized on the brutality and violence to ridicule and reject heroism. Having heard that a pilot who was transporting a portable toilet in his helicopter when it crashed, leaving him dead and buried under the toilet, one veteran said that he would like to die like that—killed by a downed toilet and buried under human excrement. "I did not want to die a heroic death," he explained.[267]

ALTERED STATES OF BEING

Since World War I, it has been generally acknowledged that a man does not have to be killed or physically wounded in war to become a casualty. Death not only destroyed bodily life in Vietnam; most often it damaged the survivors' inner selves. Post-Traumatic Stress Disorder was not in common usage at the time, but the psychological upheavals caused by the war came home with the soldiers who fought in Vietnam. Eyesight, limb, or life itself were not the only things they stood to lose.[268] Such was the power of death that simple closeness to the dosage was enough to cause damage. "Exposure to dead bodies sensitized you to the force of their presence and made for long reverberations;" a reporter who lived close to the troops on the battlefield discovered. Some were so vulnerable that one look at the dead "was enough to wipe them away." The sight could destroy whatever spirit and self-respect a soldier might have had. Even hardened veterans knew when they came close to the bodies that "something weird and extra was happening to them." [269] Death and the suffering of the dying were not random events; they were the inevitable result of the soldiering process, "Yet we, too, die," a soldier-poet wrote, "while winning such fights / From a sickness caused by slaughter." [270] That sickness could alter the functioning of the soul and its perception of reality or kill it altogether. A veteran while asleep realized this when he saw dead men living, and while awake saw living men dead. These altered states were symptoms of the shock and eventual depression that possessed him when thinking about dead comrades who had "died for nothing." Their wasted lives and futures filled the survivor with such hatred and violence that, "I even hated myself as well," he confessed, and fell "into morbid depressions and thinking about committing suicide." At other times, he felt like killing someone else.[271]

Such deviant states naturally altered one's views about war and one's role in it. They especially affected soldiers who had believed in a cause and had gone to war to serve their country. Those men had the most difficulty in confronting and coping with death. The thought of it had been far from their minds when they enlisted. Enthusiasm, eagerness to show what they could do, or the drive to quench a thirst for heroism, these things veiled the realities of the battlefield whose cruelty they could not imagine before they got there. Death's proximity generated an abhorrence that was stronger than the initial resolve that had taken shape in a time of innocence. It led them to reconsider the meaning of the war and its role in their life. Faced with the specter of pain and suffering, their beliefs faltered, and their aggressive will evaporated. Ron Kovic, the would-be hero of *Born on the Fourth of July*, wanted to prove that he was "a brave man, a good Marine." He was determined never to retreat, no matter what happened to him, "I had to be courageous," he told himself while advancing toward a Vietnamese village held by the enemy. He was hit on one foot and one shoulder, and a bullet severed his spinal cord. He became paralyzed from his chest down. The wounds shattered his outlook on heroism and life, and the cause he had believed in suddenly came to nothing. "I was frightened to death," he remembered while lying on the ground wounded, his heroic spirit silenced. "All I could feel was [that I had been] cheated. All I could feel was the worthlessness of dying right here in this place at this moment for nothing."[272] Chained to the pain that filled their body and mind, all thoughts of nobility and valor were erased forever along with the beliefs that had brought him to the war.

Lieutenant Philip Caputo, too, wanted a chance "to live heroically." When he saw the poster of an athletic Marine officer and read about the amazing deeds of the Marines, he was sure he would find in war the "heroic experience" he sought. He wanted to prove "my courage, my toughness, my manhood" in the service of his country. During training, he performed his classroom work diligently, but he was impatient for the physical battles against impossible odds, the sort of things that movies like Guadalcanal Diary and Retreat Hell! had shown him in the comfort of his living room.[273] However, when he came face to face with the realities in the field, the heroic life he believed in was sadly inadequate to sustain him. The presence of death aroused contrary forces and feelings that drowned out those that had induced him to prove his "toughness." Combat taught him the "old lessons about fear, cowardice, courage," but he was left with an "an emptiness, a sense of futility" that canceled his earlier beliefs. In between actions, he spent the time thinking about his fallen friends. They "might as well have died in automobile accidents," he brooded. If there was anything to be learned from their disappearance, it was that he was forced to face the reality of death. "We learned about death at an age when it is common to think of oneself as immortal." In civilian life, everyone gradually loses that illusion. But in Vietnam, one loses it in a matter of weeks. As a result, Caputo aged prematurely. "The knowledge of death," he recalled, cut him off from his youth in the same way a surgeon's scissors had once severed him from the womb." [274] The experience led him to contemplate suicide.

Another soldier marched to war as a proud Marine. Initially, Lieutenant Puller embraced the cause of anti-Communism and military duty. It never occurred to him that politicians and war managers could be making wrong decisions. But the wound that maimed and slowly destroyed what remained of his life radically changed his view. He realized that policies carried out by American leadership had been unwarranted. Their wrongfulness had made the soldiers' wounds and deaths "meaningless" rather than noble, "As I looked around and saw the policy brokers that were causing the deaths of American and Vietnamese boys without any consequences to themselves, I became cynical and completely distrustful of the wisdom that I had heretofore taken on faith." He had been damaged for life in a war that no longer made any sense to him. He became angry and bitter and refused to regard the loss of his legs as a worthy sacrifice made on behalf of his country [275]

Ordinary recruits, less educated and only partially aware of the reasons they had been sent to Vietnam, had less complicated crises than those who knew more. Nonetheless, the shock of death's violent presence was enough to alter their inner life forever. There was "something weird and extra" in the demeanor of the combatants after being surrounded by so much death. One reporter thought he saw in many soldiers an unusual look, "Faces of boys whose whole lives seemed to have backed up on them, they'd be a few feet away, but they'd be looking back at you over a distance you knew you'd never really cross." [276] They were alienated from themselves and their fellow human beings. An essential part of them was disappearing. The perception that they were being robbed of the best years of their lives was another of those weird and extra things that happened to them. "All the youth sucked out of the eyes, the color drawn from the skin, cold white lips… Life had made him old; he'd live out old." This was the face of one of the soldiers, the same as that of many others the reporter had seen. It was a kind of paralysis of the self. Another soldier who had seen the death of comrades who had large families at home and that of comrades who were on the verge of ending their service, wrote home in 1968, "I think that with all the death and destruction I have seen in the past week I have aged greatly." [277] At Khe Sanh death was everywhere, and youth's freshness lasted in the soldiers' faces for a short time only after they arrived at the outpost. The eyes were "always either strained or blazed-out or simply blank," offering to everyone a look of extreme fatigue or "a glancing madness."[278]

Even after having returned to civilian life, the effect of their experience never left them. They became walking tombs. One veteran was unable to recognize and regain the human space that once was his, "I have traveled to a place where the dead lie above the ground in rows and bunches. Time has gone somewhere without me. This is not my country, not my time." Heinemann's book closes with the living Dosier, as dead as his friend, Quinn. Because of their close-knit comradery in battle, Quinn's death became Dosier's death. With his other half gone, Dosier was left dried up and empty. His evolving identity (like so many young men's) was arrested by the war. He broods on his friend who was "quick and clever as anything and smart as hell… Stoned or sober or ass-whipped tired, he knew the tracks and the killing and the staying alive. I mean, he and I stood back-to-back many a night. So how come? You cover me, and I'll cover you, and we'll all go home." Buried in the cemetery at Terre Haute, Quinn's decaying corpse became Dosier's dead soul.

WASTE

Waste had a connotation independent of military performance and achievements. Such was the intensity of feeling for the loss of friends and comrades that the survivors found its loss "odious and intolerable." Implicit in this was the belief that a man's life has more value than the sacrifice he was being asked to make. When a soldier stepped on a mine and was blown to bits, he was "wasted." Mines and booby traps, for instance, accounted for almost all of the casualties in Lieutenant Caputo's company.[279] The losses were tremendous. This manner of dying almost by accident made it impossible to conceive of it as a "noble sacrifice." Caputo had first-hand knowledge of this, for he was the "accountant of corpses" for his unit. His duty was to keep records of the fallen and to send death notices to their families. He had trouble writing the notices because he perceived them to be expressions of an unspeakable human failure that should not have been reduced to a few formal words expressed as a commonplace banality; he wanted no part of it. From the lieutenant's viewpoint, the notices implicitly said to the parents that their son was killed and with him the hopes and values they had instilled in him, "How do you tell parents that all the years they had spent raising and educating their son were for nothing? Wasted."[280] Lieutenant Caputo lost the illusion that there was any good way to die in Vietnam. In his memoir, there is only a sense of irreparable, useless loss. Private Sullivan had died of a sniper's bullet while filling canteens at the edge of a river. Of course, he died in the line of duty. But duty no longer justified it. The sniper who killed him took aim on his telescopic sight, "and all that Sullivan had ever been or would ever be, all of his thoughts, memories, and dreams were annihilated in an instant." What once mattered—the thoughts, memories, and dreams of Sullivan as a man—duty had been destroyed. What now mattered was that those things had gone to waste. [281]

This squandering of life stirred the imagination of many survivors who kept their friends alive by fixing the rich humanity they represented as men, not as heroes. They transformed one soldier who was an ordinary man into an exceptional one, not because of his military deeds, but because of the human values that had been erased. Medic Walter Levy was killed while attempting to drag a wounded combatant to safety. The deed was certainly a cause for celebrating his courage. But Levy is remembered for his qualities as a human being, not as a dutiful soldier serving his country. He is remembered as a skilled and daring medic in the field, an intellectual, a philosopher, and a thinker. He and others like him who had met the same fate represented "the [ultimate] good" in people be it in war or civilian life. "What matters is that you were alive then, alive and speaking," the narrator says, unable to give up what Levy represented as a human being: talent, intelligence, and generosity, all the qualities that should not be wasted. "There are a few of us who do remember because of the small things that made us love you—your gestures, the words you spoke, and the way you looked. We loved you for what you were and what you stood for. So much was lost with you, so much talent and intelligence and decency… You embedded the best that was in us… and a part of us died with you." [282] The narrator celebrates Levy's nobility as a civilian man who in the role of a soldier lost the very qualities that not only ennobled him but also elevated those around him. If one thinks of a hero as someone who behaves selflessly at considerable personal risk to save another, Levy's deed served a worthy, though circumscribed, cause and would be considered in the minds of many to be noble, if not heroic. But in the context of a war that did not serve to make the world a better place, in a mistaken war such as the one in Vietnam, his deed had less ultimate value. How then, can courage be valued when the irrevocable sacrifice discards all that is good in people?

WHAT REMAINS

In a well-known memoir, *The Things They Carried*, by Tim O'Brien, the disappearance of dignity and self-respect that normally leads the way to courage takes on a new dimension. The death of a fallen soldier for whom O'Brien and his friend, Bowker, had a special tie, turns into an unusual experience. In an image never before having appeared in the annals of war literature, O'Brian tells of his effort to recover their comrade from a swamp of excrement, "There were bubbles where Kiowa's head should have been. . . He pulled hard, but Kiowa was gone, and then suddenly he felt himself going, too. He could taste it. The shit was in his nose and eyes. There were flares and mortar rounds—and the stink was everywhere—it was inside him, in his lungs—and he could no longer tolerate it. Not here, he thought. Not like this. He released Kiowa's boot and watched it slide away. Slowly, working his way up, he hoisted himself out of the deep mud, and then he lay still and tasted the shit in his mouth and closed his eyes and listened to the rain and explosions and bubbling sounds." That swamp of excrement had prevented him from recovering the body, "that shit field," had shown "terrible killing power." He again tried to recover the body enduring another agonizing experience in the same spot where Kiowa had disappeared. The muddy excrement becomes the hallmark of his friend's death. "He remembered grabbing the boot. He remembered pulling hard, but how the field seemed to pull it back like quicksand in a tug-of-war he could not win. Finally, he had to whisper his friend's name and let go and watch the boot slide away. Later he found himself lying on a little rise, face-up, tasting the field in his mouth, listening to the rain and explosions and bubbling sounds. He was alone." That swamp of excrement had swallowed Kiowa. The extraordinary difference between Kiowa's end and the goodness he had represented to all who knew him in life eventually produced in the survivors a new evaluation of the war. How could so much good end up drowned in the most unsavory place man can think of? During the twenty years that followed O'Brien's return to the U.S., his experience in the field of excrement gradually came to embody all "the waste that was Vietnam, all the vulgarity and horror." At the end of those twenty years, he returned to the site where he had tried in vain to recover Kiowa's body. "My best friend. My pride. My belief in myself as a man of some small dignity and courage" had disappeared. He realized that "after that long night in the rain, [he] had grown cold inside, all the illusions gone, all the old ambitions and hopes for myself were sucked away into the mud. Over the years, that coldness had never entirely disappeared. There were times . . . when I could not feel much, not sadness or pity or passion, and somehow I blamed this place for what I had become, and I blamed it for taking away the person I had once been." [283] The destructive power of death had deadened his spirit and ruined his potential for any joy in life. For O'Brien the field of shit stood for the entire war in Vietnam, but as excrement itself has fertilizing power, who is to say what might be gained for future generations from that mistaken war?

    On those combatants who were religious, the violence had the effect of undermining their belief in everlasting life. The sight of mutilated bodies, their organs splattered over the ground, and the clothes of the wounded disturbed the onlooker's belief in the living spirit. For those who were Roman Catholic, it destroyed "the religious myths" of their Catholic faith. An officer who was keeping tab of the fallen in his unit came to realize that it was impossible to look at those bloody clutters and still believe they would be capable of a bodily resurrection on judgment day, that they had souls within them that would survive to live a better life in another world. He could no longer look at the remains of those men and "still believe their souls had passed on to another existence, or that they had souls in the first place. I could not believe those bloody messes would be capable of a resurrection on the Last Day." It made no difference to these survivors whether the mutilations and scattered parts were those of hero or coward; to them, the fallen "were gone for good, body, mind, and spirit." The ugliness of the spectacle erased deeply held beliefs. When men so violated, lie like roadkill on the highways, who could believe them to be superior to the animals? We are one of them. No more or less. In death a mass of repulsive flesh and bones. Neither is there any recourse in playing the "victim" because even as the bodies festered and sank, one knew they had perpetrated the same bodily horror on the enemy. The officer recalled his response to the sight, "The horror lay in the recognition that the body, which is supposed to be the earthly home of an immortal soul... is in fact only a fragile case stuffed full of disgusting matter."[284] War and death left Christian doctrine unchanged, but in the mind and hearts of those who witnessed the senselessness of such slaughter, the doctrine made no sense.

In the Pacific arena during World War II, a soldier may also have been sickened at the sight of men wounded or killed day after day. He could be drained of emotion and strength, but at the end of the action, there was a reward. He had accomplished something "special." He had survived the intense physical exertion in unbearable muggy heat and had stood up to the enemy. The memoirs of that war reveal a great deal of fear and suffering, but also a note of pride.[285] But there was not the same overall pride in American soldiers in Vietnam who also endured extreme hardship. Their endurance came from an obsessive desire to avoid death. There was little forward motion or sense of accomplishment, only the instinct of preservation at work. Their one and only thought—to escape the death that constantly hovered over them. Their one and only cause—to survive the ordeal. Admittedly, life in all people increases in value the closer it comes to destruction, but for the soldiers in Vietnam, there was no compensatory reward.

Two psychologically opposing forces are at work as a result of fear. On the one hand, a strong desire to survive may incapacitate a soldier and wipe out his ability to respond. On the other, the same fear can unleash what is called the fighting spirit in a burst of extraordinary energy. His military spirit may take over, giving him the will power to do his best to conquer and survive. In a world where just about everything and everyone conspires to kill and destroy, survival must be the combatants' supreme goal. Such a world was Vietnam. No one regarded his possible demise to be a sacrifice for the good of his country. Such an ideal was far removed from reality. American combatants may have felt doomed, but they all clung to life. For them, death was "the Worst Thing in the World."[286] It had to be defied at all costs. Because it was the worst thing that could happen, a lofty appeal was often regarded as an obscenity. No soldier would dream of translating into reality the classical saying, "dulce et decorum est pro patria mori." For the ancients, death in battle was the ultimate, honored sacrifice; for the Americans, that aphorism would have sounded like an "epitaph for the insane." It only increased the risk of death. At death's door, there was "no valor to squander for country or honor or military objectives."[287] It was an act of madness. It is no wonder the Marines had the "twin obsession of Death and Peace."[288] The obsession for the first came from the profound wish to avoid the thing in whose proximity they were chained day and night; and for the second, from the belief that, if peace prevailed, it would spare them from being victims of the worst thing in the world and allow them to realize their wish to survive and go home. The only victory for them in Vietnam "was not to die."[289]

SURVIVAL

In the fall of 1965 when the war was still young, the soldiers already "fought for no cause other than [their] own survival." "Everything rotted and corroded quickly," they realized, and what corroded first was the will to fight for victory. They faced the enemy under the scorching sun, tormented by wind, rain, and monsoons, in swamps and jungles, places they had not known before. They knew it was nearly impossible to prevail over both the enemy and the environment, and they had little choice other than to protect themselves as best they could to keep from being destroyed. Many became ruthless as a result of this "overpowering greed for survival."[290] Survival became their highest goal. "The only thing the grunts found to win in Vietnam was 365 consecutive days of life."[291] They wanted to stay alive not for their unit or a cause, but to make sure they would make it back home. "The trick of being in Nam," many troops believed, "is getting out of Nam," not in a plastic body bag, but "alive."[292] Savage but shrewd Sergeant Sace of *The LBJ Brigade* is an expert "on staying alive" in the midst of a murderous war. Before his men would undertake a mission, he would explain to them that they were fighting neither Communists, nor Viet Cong, nor on behalf of American freedom. "You," he said, "are fighting to stay alive." [293] The will to survive often inspired a combatant to fight with valor, especially when the life of a comrade was at stake and there were many courageous acts in recovering the wounded and dead. But how well one managed to survive was less important than the motivation—a deep loathing and fear of death. Even though the soldier who fought for his own and others' survival, may have been fighting heroically, his heroism was purely a self-serving action that extended equally to his comrades with whom he identified intimately. It had nothing to do with the primary aim of the military leadership, that of conquest and victory. "We were fighting in the cruelest kind of conflict," one of its protagonists recorded, a people's war. It was not an orderly campaign as the European war had been. It was "a war for survival waged in a wilderness without rules or laws; a war in which each soldier fought for his own life and the lives of the men beside him." The greed for survival overrode all military objectives. Here a strong kind of comradery was born, a comradery that had nothing to do with patriotism, but a great deal with "taking care of each other," because "the basic idea was to stay alive."[294] Sergeant Gilliland recalled that getting out alive had been his constant worry, "It was all he had thought about for months, the major topic of conversation in the bush. Life's goals reduced to ground zero, to stay alive long enough to leave."[295] Lieutenant Caputo concludes his narrative in a way that summarizes for the combatants the meaning of their Vietnam adventure, "We had done nothing more than endure. We had survived, and that was our only victory."[296]

But all this does not mean that the Americans showed signs of cowardice or refused to fight. On the contrary, they faced the enemy with no less resolve than when they first enlisted. In the midst of pain, suffering, and death, an individual can surprisingly call on his survival instinct. The embrace of violence and destruction has its own kind of therapy; it resists death by acknowledging its presence. The "young gods" quickly aged in the circle of its sting and, though not to make light of the tragic alienation and soul destruction it caused, its concentrated presence aroused a deep craving for life that effectively animated the soldiers' martial spirit with the desire to kill whether legitimate or illegitimate. Prodded by the "body count," avoidance of death came to depend to a large extent on killing as many enemies as possible. Surviving manifested itself through a singular attachment to life, an inner persuasion of its intrinsic worth, and because its loss was so devastating to the survivors, they spoke often of the individual traits and characteristics of their dead comrades as living beings. "We had ways of making the dead seem not quite so dead" and "we kept the dead alive with stories," remembering the best they had shown when they were alive. The combatants' lives had become so valuable that their lives could not be stolen. "Once you are alive... you can't ever be dead."[297]

WHY VETERANS MISS WAR

It is ironic that one may come fully alive only when defeat and death are imminent.[298] As described earlier, the proximity of death unleashes an extraordinary excess of adrenalin and energy that has the power of "bringing you fully awake," of making "things vivid," of seeing things "you never saw before; you pay attention to the world." The risk of catastrophe may bring the "pleasure of aliveness," which makes one feel "your truest self, the human being you want to be... You love what is best in yourself and in the world, all that might be lost."[299]

Understandably, a soldier is overwhelmed with joy when he comes through a fight safely, especially when he realizes that so many around him are dead. "And yet, any soldier will tell you that the closeness to death brings with it a corresponding closeness to life. For a moment "don't think about it morally, think about it neurologically," said Sabastian Junger, a veteran journalist covering a remote outpost in Afghanistan in 2007, "What's happening in your brain is you're getting an enormous amount of adrenaline pumped through your system, and young men will go to great lengths to have that experience. It's hormonally supported."[300] When the Navy Seals in 2011, stormed the compound in Abbottabad where Osama bin Laden lived, and President Obama, watching on live video from the White House, declared, "We got him," Admiral McRaven was at first skeptical. The Seals, he said, are on a mission, and "their adrenaline is sky high." The Admiral would not draw any conclusions until the evidence was in. In fact, the high-wired Seals shot the unarmed bin Laden so many times that at first, they were unsure who he was. His face was a "mangled mess." [301]

One is never more alive than when he is almost dead. After a firefight there is always the immense pleasure of aliveness," because it is a victory against death, itself. But in the midst of so much loss, that pleasure had to be a "secret joy." [302] "And all that time Paco kept one thought in his head as distinct as a colorful dream—I must not die." He kept saying "I must not die" like a litany, as though he felt life is running out each instant that he did not say it. So too, Private Dosier lies near his wounded comrade, and the only thing he can think of and act on is warding off death: "I am whispering louder and louder into his bloody muddy face: Don't die, hey, don't die, don't die." He squeezes his hand imploring him not to die. It soon changes into a desperate command, "Live, goddamn it, live, goddamn you... All I say is live, live in tight-lipped stage whispers, louder and louder and angrier." [303] The longing for survival was deep; it transcended the boundaries of reason and became surreal.

Cause or no cause, when it came to confronting death in battle, the combatant was overwhelmed by a healthy albeit primitive instinct for survival. The mind naturally closed down, and the soldier was absorbed in the task of fighting. Thus, traction may be gained. The difficulty arises when an uncommitted soldier serves a personal rather than a military need. He is alienated from the military hierarchy and its objectives with the result that purely emotional and psychological needs easily surpass all ethical considerations often with tragic consequences. Soldiers whose single motivation is their own survival may well emerge as heroes, but not the sort of heroes the military wants to decorate and parade before the public as models to emulate

IV

THE LEGACY

It was not until I was in Iraq and reading secret military reports on a daily basis that I started to question the morality of what we were doing. I realized in our efforts to meet the risk posed to us by the enemy, we have forgotten our humanity. We consciously elected to devalue human life both in Iraq and Afghanistan[304]

A major lesson not learned from Vietnam was the proper reading of history. Historical precedent and simple reason alone should have warned Americans not to get involved in that conflict. It was essentially a civil war that should have been resolved by the Vietnamese people alone. As Bernard Fall emphasized, "It was a local conflict with outside support which had gotten out of hand, not a worldwide cold-war confrontation.[305] What American political strategists and military planners failed to grasp as they prepared to intervene following the French defeat at Dien Bien Phu in 1954 was that they were wading into an anti-colonial struggle for national independence that in the long run no outside force could stop or reverse. President Johnson, speaking at Johns Hopkins University in April 1965, in response to the question of why we needed to fight in Vietnam, replied, "We fight because we must fight if we are to live in a world where every country can shape its own destiny." Ironically, the Vietnamese people were doing just that—struggling to shape their own destiny after years of foreign domination. Indeed, the American presence in that country was based precisely on the fear that the Vietnamese *would* shape their own destiny. As an afterthought, Johnson came closer to the truth when he added, "to strengthen world order,"[306] which meant bolstering capitalistic democracy against the perceived communist threat. But the dishonesty of his statement was not lost on ordinary Americans. Cold war tension had dissipated considerably since the paranoia of the fifties, and most were loath to stir up out-worn passions. Certainly, American shores were not in danger. In retrospect, considering the many communist countries that have unraveled of their own accord, fear of North Vietnamese communism's ability to disrupt the free world far surpassed the reality. Years of western interference had brought internal dissension among differing loyalties, not the least being the resistance of traditional Buddhism to the Catholic Church that was co-joined to French rule. The complex blend of Buddhism, Confucianism, and Taoism in the political and cultural life of the Vietnamese was lost on the U.S. military and political establishment who ignored the opposition by communists and non-communists alike to the Catholic government of Ngo Dinh Diem. This blindness was typical of the proselytizing effort of Americans to convert and westernize non-Christian peoples. "From 1954 onward, Francis Cardinal Spellman declared that Vietnam was vital to the preservation of Catholicism and the American way of life." [307] He promoted the belief that Vietnam was a Catholic nation when in fact, it was and still is predominately Buddhist.

Similarly, in the Middle East, America has either misread or not understood an Islamic culture riddled with sectarian rivalries, or respected the conflicting interests among the religious sects. For example, having disregarded the budding al-Qaeda among Saudi men in her undaunted support of the Saudi family, she was astonished to discover that Saudi nationals had piloted the surprise attack on the World Trade Center in September 2001. The event prompted Susan Sontag to famously note in the New Yorker of that week, that the attack was "a consequence of specific American alliances and actions," adding that "America has never seemed farther from an acknowledgment of reality than it has been in the face of last Tuesday's monstrous dose of reality."[308] Worse was the later misreading of information about Iraq's atomic arsenal that led to the U.S. invasion of that country. In the words of Andrew Bacevich, "the Iraq war ranks as the most consequential foreign policy failure since Vietnam." [309]

Most people have scant enthusiasm for war, and it is hard for governments to drum up the energy for such an undertaking, especially against foreign countries about which one knows little if anything. To gather sufficient forces, governments must entice citizens with money and other benefits to get them to enlist, or if enticements don't work, they conscript. Conscription was a ball and chain on the majority of men sent to Vietnam. In 1963 the Selective Service Board needed 35,000 a month. Some were willing volunteers, but as the war progressed, the burgeoning resistance brought home the inner conflict between the lack of commitment and the necessity of serving. By 1972, public protests were rampant throughout the nation. Some 200,000 to 500,000 refused to pay excise taxes on their telephone bills. Another 20,000 were resisting all or part of their income taxes. Thousands fled to Canada. After Vietnam, American leaders prudently abandoned compulsory military service for a voluntary one. In a free society when military solutions are resorted to, the wisdom of establishing a draft should be carefully examined. The draft is a two-edged sword. Patriotic obedience and critical thinking do not necessarily converge toward a common goal. When agreeably wedded and fairly administered the draft is the most democratic method of obtaining military service. But to court "the red animal," when there is no collective unity among the people, the implementation of a draft is certain to fuel a strong protest movement.

Notwithstanding the exhaustive political and historical analysis of the war that appeared in the years following 1975, what truly matters for this study are the individual traumas, the sacrifices, and futures needlessly denied. For one might easily gloss over the statistics: 58,195 Americans dead and roughly 304,000 wounded and maimed for life. Even more tragic was the cost to the Vietnamese people. More than 2 million Vietnamese died in the war, and the country was left in tatters—the land scattered with mines, chemical residue, and other dangers lurking in the shadows. Many

Vietnamese historical sites and buildings were destroyed and millions were left homeless.[310] Unfortunately, human nature being what it is, people not personally connected to the dead or struggling veterans, or the Vietnamese, are not easily moved by mere numbers. Such are the forms of loss throughout history—cities burnt, ships sunk, whole armies destroyed. But no matter how wide its implications for a community or state, tragedy is measured by the defeat and destruction of the solitary human figure, soldier or civilian. Thus, in this country, as we contemplate the Vietnam Veterans Memorial Wall in Washington, the proper feeling can only be that of grief and sorrow. Secretary McNamara and others tried to soften the personal losses for the families left behind by declaring their sons' sacrifices to be a noble and honorable act while at the same time admitting that the war in Vietnam was an unworthy undertaking.[311] What else could he say without admitting to those bereft that the sacrifices had been a terrible waste? Contrary to his declaration, the traditional value placed on sacrifice has been severely tarnished by the unworthiness of the enterprise. On the other hand, not in vain were the sacrifices made by the Viet Cong soldiers. They are finally at peace in a unified Vietnam, a communist Vietnam; it was what they wanted after years of subjugation to colonial rule.

A recent series of interviews of a few surviving Vietnamese veterans was conducted by a group of American college students who traveled to Vietnam in an effort to understand how, fifty years after the war, the Vietnamese of today think about the War. They found these men, now in their sixties and seventies, to be amazingly compassionate toward Americans. As one veteran said, "I know that it was the American government, and that these American boys did not want to come to Vietnam. How were they so different than myself, young and unaware?" Another veteran said, "The image we had of Americans was that they were the creators of death and destruction. They ruled the skies, and we were constantly hiding in caves. We knew we were probably going to die, and we felt like we'd rather keep on going, keep on fighting for the unification of our country. We were fighting the good war."[312]

Though a just cause collectively supported is the foundation of success in war, one should not infer that failure in battle is always due to an unworthy cause. An indigenous army of resistance up against a powerful invading force invariably needs outside support. If the Viet Cong had not had military advisors from China, they might not have prevailed no matter how justified their cause. One need only reflect at length on the American Revolution, and how it might have been lost without the help of France. Even so, it is the worthiness of the cause that ennobles the sacrifice. A soldier profoundly committed to something beyond himself can turn death into "a mere happenstance." It was thus that the North Vietnamese could defy death and turn it into a mark of valor.

NEW WARS

Many people hoped that America's failure in Vietnam might bring about a renewal of sorts, that in the future a careful consideration of the consequences of going to war over the slightest provocation would induce strict scrutiny before asking the ultimate from the nation's youth. Alas, this has hardly been the case. Since the end of that war, the United States has embroiled itself in three successive military conflicts and is presently engaged in a fourth.

The Persian Gulf War (August 1990—February 1991) was endorsed and aided by UN Security Council Resolution 678 which demanded Iraq's withdrawal from Kuwait. It was of short duration and carried out by a volunteer army for very practical reasons; namely, to keep Kuwait's oil flowing to the west. Oil being the lifeblood of the American economy, many would argue this to have been sufficient reason. Fortunately, it ended at Iraq's border. Then, only eight years later, the U.S. was engaged in another military conflict, one not authorized by the UN Security Council—the NATO attack on Serbia and ten weeks of bombing Kosovo. Although the unilateral use of force constituted a violation of the UN Charter, the U.S. State Department cited human rights abuses as justification for the bombing. As a result of the collateral damage that included the Chinese embassy in Belgrade, Chinese Premier Jiang Zemin declared that the U.S. was using its economic and military strength to aggressively expand its influence and interfere in the internal affairs of other countries.[313]

The attack on the World Trade Center in New York in September 2001 by Saudi terrorists working for Al Qaeda was the rationale for two more U.S.-led invasions. The audacity and force of the attack took America by surprise and understandably caused strong emotions to arise. While it was known among intelligent sources, who masterminded the attack and why, the plan to have Osama bin Laden arrested and tried by an international tribunal of Islamic leaders was blocked by President Musharraf of Pakistan, who said that he couldn't guarantee bin Laden's safe passage; whereupon the U.S. threatened to bomb Afghanistan. The Taliban ambassador, Abdaul Salam Zaeef pleaded in vain, "We do not want to compound the problems of the people, the country, or the region. The Afghan people need food, need aid, need shelter, not war." [314] The U.S. refused, and in spite of the fact that the U.N. Security Council would not authorize the action because the U.S. had no proof that the attack was connected to the Afghan nation or the Taliban government and therefore could not constitute self-defense, on October 7, 2001, the U.S. began an aerial bombing campaign. There were two more attempts by the Taliban to negotiate a transfer of bin Laden provided the U.S. would stop the bombing, but again, as happened in 1965 to the chance for a negotiated peace in Vietnam, the U.S. rejected every offer in the belief that a military strike would bring that country to its heels. Several experts on Afghan affairs noted that the U.S. missed its chance for a satisfactory settlement. [315] Once the violence began, the United Nations authorized an International Security Assistance Force to help the Afghans maintain security in the region around Kabul. Initially, the Taliban retreated into the mountains, but the continued bombing and eventual addition of troops on the ground caused the Taliban to grow in numbers until it comprised a hardcore of highly motivated insurgents surrounded by many alienated young Afghans angered by the bombing raids or in return for money. Soon, foreign nationals joined in sympathy with the insurgents. According to officials, most of them were from Pakistan, Uzbekistan, Chechnya, and various Arab countries, even Turkey and western China. [316] Neighboring Pakistan's complicity with both sides of the civil and religious factions has made that country a target of terrorism and general mayhem—a classic example of the consequences of repeated American heavy-handedness and cultural myopia in the application of military and foreign policy. It is what the late political scientist Chalmers Johnson called "blowback," with the predictable effect of alienating the allies and the people they are wanting to help.

Next, the Bush administration added fuel to the fear of more attacks from the Islamic world by announcing to the nation that Iraq (not having signed the nuclear non-proliferation pact) was developing weapons of mass destruction. It is not a stretch of the imagination to conclude that the March 2003 invasion of Iraq was an angry wish by the President to continue the Persian Gulf War that had been wisely stopped at the Iraq border by his father, H.W. Bush. The invasion was strongly opposed by America's European allies since there was no evidence to support the charge that Saddam Hussein was harboring nuclear weapons. But fear and revenge were in the air, and many in the U.S. were primed for action and eager to give the junior Bush carte blanche to repay Hussein's former belligerency. The invasion was based on false intelligence and therefore had no legitimate cause. There were no weapons of mass destruction and no evidence that Iraq harbored Al Qaeda terrorists. Had there been a draft at the time, no doubt, there would have been a national backlash, especially after the truth became known.

Quick to show her muscle, the U.S. continues to act with few restraints. For much of the rest of the world, her willingness to display her military might whenever and wherever she thinks her interests are threatened is a cause for dismay. Names like Abu Ghraib, Guantanamo, and Bagram hardly engender respect for her mission in the world. Rather, they induce fear and loathing. Instead of reducing the threat of terrorism, they increase the chance of "blowback" when the very mention of such names adds desperate and impressionable young men to join the ranks of would-be terrorists. No one in Washington understood the complicated religious and sectarian rivalries that for years sustained an uneasy peace in Iraq. The invasion succeeded in stirring up this delicate balance and completely destroying the infrastructure of that country. Repercussions among civilians whose lives and welfare have been disrupted or tragically ended, ripen the ranks of future enemies such as the Islamic State of Iraq and Syria and the newly fortified Taliban, and exacerbated the ethno-sectarian struggles that have historically been part of the Arab culture. "Force is good for defending what is already yours," writes Andrew Bacevich, professor of international relations at Boston University "but not content to merely defend its own, the U.S. in recent decades has sought to use force to extend its influence, control, and values on others ... Expecting coercion to produce acceptance or submission, represents the height of folly, and force employed in far-away places serves to inflame further resistance."[317] The continued presumption of American omnipotence and the hubris it carries to the rest of the world, especially to the weaker, struggling states of the third world where resentment among people who proudly hold to their traditions, breeds the very groups whose defining cause is to maintain their way of life against outside interference.

A major lesson not learned is that once troops are sent and blood begins to flow, backing out of an action is always, resisted. Why? Because to admit a miscarriage of trust after dedicated lives have been destroyed or wounded is almost impossible. Mitt Romney exemplified this inclination during the presidential campaign of 2012 when he said that any pullout from Iraq would "unnecessarily put at risk the victories won through the blood and sacrifice of thousands of American men and women." [318] It remains to be seen what he meant by "victories," since other than toppling Hussein from power, there were none. At risk was the realization that thousands of Americans had died for no good reason or worthwhile cause. Similarly, the Bush administration, at the height of violence in Iraq, argued that abandoning a commitment to stabilize the country would squander former U.S. sacrifices on the battlefield. While it is right and just to remain in order to restore and stabilize a country left in chaos, it does not turn an unworthy enterprise into a worthy one, nor justify the sacrifices made.

In the wake of a classified intelligence report that the Afghan war was mired in stalemate, Rep Schakowsky (D. Ill) said: "Given the expense and the lives that are at stake, the American people should see a [unclassified] version of the top-line conclusions of this (NIE) report." [319] The Al Qaeda training camp no longer operates as before; its cells are mostly dispersed or meshed with Taliban sympathizers or hidden in other countries, and the hunt for bin Laden has been successfully concluded with his assassination on May 2, 2011. Thus, to remain in Afghanistan is to unnecessarily prolong an unworthy war now carried on by half-hearted soldiers backed by an apathetic public. Nothing much has changed the strategy that prevailed fifty years ago in Vietnam. Just as Washington once supported the unpopular government of Ngo Dinh Diem, it now backs the fragile, corrupt government of Afghan President Karzai in order to prevent the Taliban from taking over the country. The training of Afghan troops to carry the burden against opposing factions has posed the same problem as that which existed in Vietnam when training and weapons could not supply the South Vietnamese Army (ARVN) with the will to fight, because the internal conflict was not primarily military; it was a political conflict for the allegiance of the people.[320]

Understandably, the Afghans and Iraqis are increasingly hostile to the American presence. The family bonds of ordinary people whose simple lives have been turned upside down by well-meaning Americans are clearly shown in a documentary that chronicles the deployment in 2007-2008 of a platoon of U.S. soldiers in Afghanistan's Korengal Valley. The Americans were looking for Taliban strongholds in the mountains and urging the people living in the surrounding hamlets to help them push out the insurgency. But there were family ties, and when Americans took away a young man who tells them he would be killed if he were to reveal anything about the Taliban, there was an unpleasant confrontation at the weekly Shura meeting with the elders of the community. In an attempt to mollify them, Captain Kearney, the platoon leader, talked about all the good things Americans could do to give them a better life, like building a much-needed road to connect them to a larger city, but understandably the Afghans' concern was not for a new road, but the man taken prisoner, and for a cow that the soldiers had killed. "Being positive is no help," one of the soldiers complained, "when we talk about all the good things we can do for them, they don't seem to care." This is typical of American naivete. It reflects the distance of the western mind from the religious sensibilities and traditional ways of other peoples, a lack of understanding that not only defeats their military goal but points to the absurdity of the enterprise in the first place. A proud people, the Afghans can't help but feel patronized.[321] In 2010, unable to excise the Taliban, the platoon was withdrawn from the valley.

Another tragic encounter with the Afghan people occurred one night in the province of Gardez in 2009. In spite of the information from his

National Security Adviser, James Jones, that "the al Qaeda presence is very diminished, and that Afghanistan is not in imminent danger of falling," President Obama, under the influence of his generals, announced a surge in Afghanistan. It meant an increase in U.S. Troops from 68,000 to 100,000. "Their goal was to disrupt, dismantle, and defeat al Qaeda, and ... to reverse the Taliban momentum." Under this new dictum, the pace of night raids accelerated, as did the list of people to be killed. "This created an atmosphere in which a tremendous number of innocent Afghans found themselves facing US commandos bursting into their homes in the middle of the night snatching or killing people."[322] On one of these night raids, masked commandos burst into the home of a respected police officer during a christening party for his newborn child. The soldiers killed the police officer, his brother, and three women. "My father was friends with the Americans, and they killed him, the police officer's son told a journalist covering the story. "They killed my father. I want to kill them. I want the killers brought to justice." Several people witnessed the soldiers digging bullets out of the women's bodies, to remove the proof that would contradict the eventual cover-up. In the end, the truth did come out, and General McChrystal and vice Admiral McRaven, head of JSOC, apologized to the family and offered them money, but the anger of the family had hardened, "I don't accept their apology. I would not trade my sons for the whole kingdom of the United States," the father stated. "Initially, we were thinking that Americans were the friends of Afghans, but now we think that Americans themselves are terrorists." The father of one of the women killed added, "We call them the American Taliban."[323]

In Iraq, ten years of relentless violence has left the cradle of civilization demolished, its museums and monuments looted, its infrastructure destroyed, and a high proportion of its population scattered, leaving the country to face an uncertain future of social re-building in a context of sectarian discord. Except for the fact that a draft on American men has not been imposed (a fact, no doubt, that has prevented a repeat of the massive protests that occurred during the Vietnam conflict), the U.S. has been replaying in Iraq and Afghanistan the same role she played fifty years ago in Vietnam.

BROKEN LIVES

Because it appears the U.S. has learned little or nothing from the disaster that was Vietnam and the horrendous sacrifices made by volunteer soldiers who went from idealistic enthusiasm to cynical disillusion, it is hoped that by illuminating the human consequences of war as an instrument of U.S. foreign policy, its curtailment will become essential to the nation. In these new asymmetrical wars as in that earlier one, the psychic disruptions to men who are unable to carry the burden of the military leadership's prescription to kill without guilt or anxiety, contradict the official line of America's virtuous intervention in foreign countries. The official causes, whether the "domino theory" in Vietnam or the "stabilization" of internal conflicts in Iraq and Afghanistan have not deeply taken hold in the hearts and minds of the individual combatant. Soldiers rarely fight winningly for such abstract causes. In battle, they are motivated by personal reasons such as fear and the need to survive or to avenge the deaths of their comrades. As members of an invading force fighting in unfamiliar territory against an alien culture, fear and the need to survive merge both collectively in military units and individual soldiers. An indigenous, un-uniformed opponent using guerrilla tactics may easily engender the idea that anyone could be an enemy and that everyone is an enemy, including old men, women, and children. To be constantly surrounded by death and destruction changes a man's nature and the dark side blossoms. Even those "ideal soldiers" such as the Navy Seals, who are able to carry the burden of killing, who, in fact, crave the action, are in danger of becoming permanently unfit for civilian life.

In a recent article that appeared in The Sun, Elliott Woods, a veteran of the war in Iraq who has been covering Afghanistan as a photographer and writer since 2009, has found the same turmoil and inner anxiety that disturbed the former combatants in Vietnam to be equally and tragically present in the young Marines presently engaged against the Taliban in Afghanistan. At Patrol Base Fires in Sangin, he writes, "the mostly nineteen and twenty-year-old Marines had seen enough violence to permanently line their boyish faces." One Marine, Lance Corporal John

Bohlinger described Sangin as 'a lot like Vietnam mixed with Kansas'—a firefight in a minefield, set against a backdrop of beanstalks and head-high corn, with low slung khaki-colored mountains on the horizon." Another corporal pointed to the grievous effect that violence and death had on the new recruits. "I was in Iraq three times and here one time. So, I came to this already knowing what to expect. The [new] guys had no fucking idea. When we took our mass casualties, I had to control everybody and try to calm them down." The lack of any deeply felt cause is brought home by another corporal, who, after having been wounded returned to the battlefield only "because of the guys that I'm out here with. This really isn't my fight. This really isn't America's fight either. We're kind of just here." [324]

As in Vietnam, there are examples in these new wars of degradation and craziness among American troops. Psychotic breaks were not rare occurrences. The realization that they were making no headway and that the native population hates them, is a lethal combination. In such an atmosphere, the powerful weaponry at one's disposal easily brought out the bully in them. A recent video of four Marines urinating on the corpses of Afghans, along with the killing of unarmed civilians and keeping their body parts as trophies are just two such instances. No doubt, Marine Corps Commandant, General James Amos has either forgotten or is unaware of similar Marine behavior in Vietnam when he stated that "such behavior . . . is wholly inconsistent with the high standards of conduct and warrior ethos that we have demonstrated throughout our history."[325] Really? Desecration of the dead by the soldiers in Vietnam was common. It served to placate death anxiety and indicated an exceptional thirst for stamping out the fear that gripped them. When constantly surrounded by death, various perversions have a cathartic effect. How could General Amos have overlooked the thousands of albums consisting of plastic pages with pictures of enemy corpses or body parts, severed headshots, or whole necklaces made of ears, called "love beads." Those mementos of the war in Vietnam were among the Marines' favorite keepsakes.[326]

Similar indiscriminate killings have appeared in the news. In one of the closely guarded secrets of the war uncovered in the town of Haditha, Iraq, was the 2005 massacre by Marines of twenty-four Iraqi civilians including an old man in a wheelchair, women, and children, their bodies beheaded and throats slit. Nor has the training of recruits changed from that earlier war. Marines are not told they need to identify individual targets as threatening when assaulting a hostile structure; the soldiers in Haditha were under orders to "clear the house."

On March 11, 2012, seventeen villagers, women and children included, in rural Kandahar province were gunned down in the dead of night ostensibly at the hands of a lone U.S. Army Staff Sargeant. One Afghan farmer had all eleven members of his family killed in the shooting. The killings brought forth an impassioned plea from Afghan President, Hamid Karzai for the immediate withdrawal of international forces from all rural villages in Afghanistan.[327] The American soldier "was a thirty-eight-year-old father of two small children whose civilian life … was marked by Army potlucks, Sunday brunches with his in-laws and a Disney cruise with his wife and children."[328] The report sent a retired Navy captain, Thomas Amerson, back to the history books to explore other stains on America's military history, including the 1968 massacre of Vietnamese civilians in the village of My Lai. "Too often, he argued, Americans absolve the leaders who start the wars and invest full responsibility on the combatants themselves. . ."[329] Captain Amerson's point is well taken. In truth, Gallup polls have shown that most people "view the military's senior leaders as something close to infallible." When things go wrong, citizens lay the blame entirely on Washington, when in fact inept leadership by American generals is equally responsible. In a recent article in the Defense Monitor, one of the army's own brass decries its senior leaders' "aggressive resistance to the reporting of problems, suppression of failed test results, public declarations of success where none were justified, and the absence of accountability."[330] A debate has been raised between those who would hold the Army Staff Sargeant wholly responsible for the murder, and those who feel he alone should not bare the blame. For it should be noted that in the charged environment of unending violence, psychotic breaks occur with more frequency than one cares to admit.

Others in the debate, like the 25-year veteran writing on Time magazine's blog site, would increase the military by means of a draft, arguing that the soldiers are being overused, that an all-volunteer Army was designed as a peacetime force and was never supposed to carry us through 20 years of war. This may be true, but as a means to increase the number of soldiers in a war not supported by the general population, conscription would surely invite a repeat of the turmoil that in years past caused havoc. It would reveal the wrongful nature of the enterprise.

In his essay, Murder is not an Anomaly in War, Chris Hedges has laid out the ugly reality of these asymmetrical wars "where the enemy is elusive and rarely seen, where the cultural and linguistic disconnect makes every trip outside the wire a visit to hostile territory;" such wars "feed the culture of atrocity," he writes. "The psychological leap to murder is short, and murder happens every day in Afghanistan. The Afghans hate us for our murderous rampages. They hate us for our hypocrisy." [331] In Afghanistan and Iraq, as a result of more than ten years of military action, starvation, disease, exposure, crime, and general lawlessness among civilians are rampant. An interview with a woman in Kabul revealed that safety and stability were what she and everyone craved, that her life was more stable with the hated Taliban in control than it is at present with Americans stirring things up.[332] It may be hard to pinpoint exactly what set off the American soldier at Kandahar, but enough information from various battlefields both past and present has shown that desperation, vengeance, accumulated tours of duty, and sickness all contribute to the killing instinct. As one veteran of the Vietnam war recalled, "Everybody gets hit and the hate builds up. . . He "really loved fucking killing" It soothed his pain. [333]

MORAL BURDEN

Again, Americans have been struggling in hostile terrain. The veiled women, prayer rugs, mosques, poverty, and regional factionalism mean little or nothing to the young, inexperienced soldiers, who have no knowledge of the language and history, and can demonstrate little understanding or empathy for the civilian population. The general resentment among the people has made it difficult for them to distinguish friend from foe, and the strain and uncertainty have traumatized them. Moreover, the war's present impasse brings out either of two characteristics in a soldier, the propensity to kill for sheer pleasure, or a weakening of the resolve to fight and the inevitable consequences. Under these circumstances, should the sloughing of the mores of civilization be held against them? To know the difference between what is false and what is true, what is necessary, and what in the long run is useless, in short, the moral burden should rightfully fall on the decision-makers in Washington and the commanding officers in the field. For, as one Vietnam combat veteran said, "The mortal dependence of the modern soldier on the military organization for everything he needs to survive is as great as a small child on his or her parents." [334] A young soldier is desperate for guidance. Without a higher cause, he is in mortal danger, not just of losing his body, but, indeed, his very soul. Such was the "horrific screw-up" [335] by Army Ranger leaders in the Afghanistan mountains in splitting up their platoon in April 2004. The division caused the death from "friendly fire" of Pat Tillman and the still resonating mental anguish of Steven Elliott who mistakenly shot and killed him during a firefight.

The dilemma of maintaining rules of conduct during a war waged against a guerrilla force is extensively laid out in the Australian film, Breaker Morant, which was based on a true incident at the end of the Boer War (1899-1902). Three Australian soldiers are on trial for having murdered seven prisoners and for the assassination of a German missionary. The film brings to light the moral ambiguity of a conflict entered into and fought for less than worthy goals. The battle took place at the height of British imperialism when England was intent on driving the Dutch out of South Africa in order to develop the rich gold deposits that had been discovered on their land. In 1902, Morant would not have questioned the justice of England's colonial empire or the reason for the war. He joined for the adventure and the risk. The Boers were indigent farmers who of necessity used guerrilla tactics (night raids and ambushes) to defend their land. Two pertinent and enduring facts arose during the trial—the great complexities in "charging active-duty soldiers with murder during battle," and the accountability of a soldier's commanding officer for his guidance in war. The defense counsel argued in defense of the same tragedy that has befallen Staff Sargent Bales in Afghanistan, Lieutenant Calley in Vietnam, and many other soldiers who squandered themselves in these asymmetrical wars, "that. . . horrors are committed by normal men in abnormal situations, situations in which the ebb and flow of everyday life have departed and have been replaced by a constant round of fear, anger, blood, and death." [336]

Leaving aside the political situation and consequent trial, Morant's battlefield behavior was an example of killing in a foreign war in which he had no real stake or overriding cause, a war entered into from sheer adventurism. Similarly, many soldiers today have become so desensitized and inured to the killing that they have fired on civilians deliberately while their fellow soldiers snapped pictures! Or, they fired on one another. In September 2011, two soldiers of the 3d Battalion 15th infantry regiment died after an argument in the barracks in which a third soldier pulled his weapon and started shooting.[337] While the American national conscience can maintain an uneasy peace knowing that present-day soldiers of their own free will made the choice to enlist, and most of the public can comfortably go about its business, still, a generous spirit of understanding is due to the hapless volunteers who have naively endangered their souls for unworthy causes and a tarnished heroism.

WAR CHANGES A MAN'S NATURE

The U.S. is once again receiving individual stories of returning soldiers. Tales of murder and suicide, of the homeless and maimed, stories of permanently damaged men from these wars.

Rarely acknowledged is the fact that even for those who manage to escape death or serious bodily injury, the battle experience changes a man's nature. "War," as a writer and cultural historian Louis Menand noted, "is especially terrible not because it destroys human beings, who can be destroyed in plenty of other ways, but because it turns human beings into destroyers." [338] It can easily turn a good man into a psychopath. That is what happened to Itzcoatl Ocampo who returned deeply troubled and ended up on a murderous rampage against the homeless people in Orange County, California.[339] Another Iraq veteran with PTSD, Joshua Stepp, slammed the face of his ten-month-old daughter into the floor and stuffed wet toilet paper into her throat until she died.[340] There have been countless suicides. Juliette Kayyem, writing for the Boston Globe, has reported that "the most recent Defense Department data for the years between 2005 and 2010 showed that service members on active duty take their lives at a rate of one every 36 hours. Meanwhile, the VA estimates that a veteran dies by suicide every 80 minutes. Veterans represent one percent of the population, but 20 percent of all suicides."[341] These are living testimonies of how such fruitless wars morally and physically degrade individual soldiers and increase the suffering and hostility of innocent people.

Finally, it is fitting here to bring to mind one of the many testimonials from Vietnam of fifty years ago. At the end of Larry Heinemann's novel, the newly discharged soldier, Philip Dosier, tries to buy a bottle of scotch at a cut-rate liquor store in Chicago. When the clerk will not accept his driver's license for identification (It expired while he was in the army), nor his citation for the Combat Infantryman's Badge, nor his sergeant's promotion, and refuses to sell, Dosier can barely contain his anger. He cautions himself, "Just remember, no hassle, no trouble, keep it quiet even though your heart is pounding like a madman at steel doors. . . There was no use telling that guy what I was thinking, that two days before I would have cut him in half, wrecked the store –bottles, picture windows, and all. I sat in the car shaking." Having once tapped "that swift, rush of anger" and the destruction it unleashed on the battlefield, Dosier, aka Heinemann, would struggle to control it for the rest of his life.[342]

CONVENTIONAL WAR VS ASYMMETRICAL WAR

One needs to consider the fact that these are new wars in a new age in which the rules as previously known no longer apply. In the context of what is termed asymmetrical warfare, in which the weaker, and possibly indigenous force resorts to guerrilla tactics, the standard rules of engagement no longer apply. Those traditional rules, which still form an essential part of a soldier's training, once provided him with a certain moral framework, one that held the soldier internally intact and supported his fighting with a sense of honor and fair play. This was true even when there was no deeply felt commitment on the part of the individual combatant. But such rules and constraints, which the enemy seems not to recognize or respect, and where that enemy is both elusive and quite different in appearance from oneself, are swiftly abandoned with predictable consequences. It is, therefore, understandable that American soldiers use tactics that defy the military code. If, for example, the indigenous army uses civilian homes or settlements as military bases, the success of the insurgency would depend on the American's obedience to the corresponding law that prohibits it. Thus, the temptation for Americans to break the law outright, or officially declare it null and void is enormous.[343] The commander of American forces in Haditha was unimpressed by the massacre in 2005, saying that it was the cost of doing business, and that he didn't feel the need to investigate because "they were part of a continuing pattern of civilian deaths."[344] In another incident, a Marine Staff Sargeant shot five Iraqi men without provocation, then asked a Marine to lie to investigators and say the five were slain while trying to run away.[345] No insurgent enemy or weapons were found in that house.

Native insurgents do not see themselves as guerrillas (though they certainly use the tactics, of melting into the crowd or disappearing into the familiar landscape). They see themselves as nationalists and freedom fighters with rights and history on their side. The invading soldiers may be told by their commanders that they came to liberate a country from a tyrannical system, but from the point of view of the native population, they are usurpers, imperialists, and crusaders.

Here we have a conundrum. Although war has always been the exclusive territory of unbridled violence, it depended, at least in eighteenth and nineteenth-century warfare, on a metaphysical scaffolding, something called good sportsmanship or fair-mindedness. Even before such rules of combat were formalized, bravery was acknowledged only when fights were equally matched in strength, or (as in the Spanish bull ring) puny man was pitted against the largest and most ferocious animals. There was no glory in killing a rabbit, child, or disabled human. Moreover, in those formal wars of the eighteenth and nineteenth centuries, it was primarily the combatants that suffered; whereas now the suffering falls chiefly on the civilian population. Modern warfare practically defines formlessness. It is difficult if not impossible to construct an edifice of regulations and have them followed in the midst of a war that borders on anarchy. This fact paradoxically returns our study to its original thesis: that in war, but especially in modern warfare, the worthiness of the cause is decisive not only in supporting the fighting spirit and the outcome of the endeavor but also in the self-esteem and personal integrity of the soldier. A combatant who cannot at least depend on the traditional rules of honor and fair play must have a deeply felt reason for being in that war. If not, he is lost to personal tragedy and permanent degradation. The fact that lawful and proper conduct is difficult to implement in a guerrilla war, should not mean that glory is automatically ascribed to soldiers (as it was in Vietnam) who, merely swept up by battle lust, or overtaken by personal emotions such as fear and revenge, do a lot of killing.

HEROISM AND THE HEROIC IDEAL

Recalling a poster in his local post office, entitled, 'Our American Heroes,' William Astore, a retired U.S. Air Force lieutenant colonel turned history professor, noted that ever since September of 2001, there has been a general increase in homage to the military service, "an almost religious veneration of U.S. service members and to elevate its members to hero status. Such advertising ensures that the brutalizing effects of war will be played down. A hero, he writes, "is someone who behaves selflessly, usually at considerable personal risk and sacrifice, to comfort or empower others and to make the world a better place."[346] There are many unrecognized heroes throughout society toiling against adversity in ordinary life with selfless courage and stoicism. Single mothers, homemakers, and fathers, who go about the ordinary tasks of maintaining and holding together home and family, who lay the foundation of civilized life. And as all foundations are hidden from sight, so their small, accumulated sacrifices are unsung outside their personal circle. One, of these, was the mother of William

Astore, who "raised five kids and endured without complaint the ravages of cancer... In refusing to rail against her fate" he states, "she set an example of selfless courage and heroism." [347] Life itself tests and forges real courage, and the tasks necessary to live bravely from day to day can prepare men and women for the harshest experiences. In reaching out into society to help the less fortunate, there is heroism. Nurses and doctors in emergency rooms, teachers and social workers, and members of organizations focused on aid, both for the human and the natural world on which humans depend, may come under this heading. Such spiritual and ethical values demand a different kind of strength, that of mind and soul united to an empathetic nature.

The above qualities were not the original model of what should comprise heroes and heroines. The rudiments of the heroic ideal can be traced to what Claude Levi-Strauss called the "mind in its untamed state," a state not necessarily relegated to the distant past, but one that can co-exist at any time with its counterpart, "the mind cultivated or domesticated for the purpose of yielding a return." [348] Primitive man was distinguished by his sense of absolute equality with the natural world. This amalgamation with the natural forces made him at once impersonal as the natural world and as personal as his inner nature. His mind worked purely from the material and concrete. Everything both material and immaterial had line, body, and form, and entities such as the soul and spirit could be transported, when necessary, from one place to another. The soul was the essential man inside the man. In war it was believed that the animating spirit functioned more effectively without the soul which the warrior removed from his body to place in the hands of a loved one for safe keeping before battle, thus leaving his spirit free to function as the impersonal agent of nature with all its wild fierceness and strength. Afterward, the warrior could recover his soul and become fully human again. Should he die in battle, his spirit would be recycled in the memories of his descendants. Thus, the deeds of a great warrior lived so long as they were remembered. This animistic thinking is basic to the original heroic ideal and the immortality achieved by the heroes of the late Bronze Age.[349] Glorified in life and mythologized after death, their battles made them the marvels of their age, but they were, for the most part, self-serving—to dazzle the world with their awe-inspiring strength, to cause fear and thereby gain eternal fame.

Even though physical prowess, a material quality without any ethical or spiritual value was honored in the ancient world, the Greeks knew that their heroes (with the exception of Ulysses) were notoriously hot-tempered and rather stupid. They acted out of pure emotion with little or no presence of mind and could cause unnecessary and terrible harm in equal proportion to good. Achilles' anger is the subject of the *Iliad*. His heartless revenge on Hector for the death of his friend and comrade in arms, Patroclus, is well known. The reprimand by Apollo begins the final chapter of that epic poem:

> "A lion, not a man, who slaughters wide,
> In strength of rage, and impotence of pride;
> Who hastens to murder with a savage joy,
> Invades around and breathes but to destroy!
> Shame is not of his soul; nor understood,
> The greatest evil and the greatest good.
>
> * * * *
>
> Brave though he be, yet by no reason awd,
> He violates the laws of man and god." [350]

Still, anyone versed in ancient civilizations knows that in the convergence of art and life, the seeds of psychological awareness and ethical considerations were germinating. While the Greek heroes were greatly admired for their courage and bravery, there is everywhere running through classical literature the theme of insanity, of a hero's mind, running amok, and its tragic effects. In literature as in life, their emotions swung between terrible madness and the abyss of remorse. Hercules' madness caused him to kill his wife and three sons. "What is this journey that you make?" Asks his father. "Has the blood of those you've slain made you mad?" When his senses return, and he realizes what he has done, Hercules, cries out, "The man who would prefer great strength more than love, more than friends, is diseased of soul." [351] Over six thousand years ago in the Mesopotamian city of Uruk (modern-day Iraq) and mythologized in what is perhaps the oldest story in the world, human compassion and ethical consideration are anticipated in the legend of a historical king who from arrogance and hubris, arrived at the ability to control his wild, indifferent spirit and to finally rule himself and his people without violence, selfishness, or the compulsions of a restless heart, his name, Gilgamesh.

WAR AND THE SOUL

Because in civilized nations humanity is strong and the warrior spirit weak, Clausewitz preached the necessity of developing what civilization has put in abeyance. War itself, he believed, is the main tool for bringing men back to their primitive state. Ferocious, uninhibited fighting and ruthless killing require the same impersonal spirit that exists in nature. This is why special units such as the Green Berets and the Navy Seals stand apart from other soldiers. Their identity as men depends to a large degree on their physical prowess. They are imbued with the martial spirit and dedicated to violence. As a consequence, they are inclined to find civilian life boring and intolerable in times of peace, and they would therefore remain at the disposal of the military. Unlike these special units, however, the majority of veterans after serving in the field, struggle valiantly and often in vain with their "diseased souls." The mind having breached all civilized boundaries, does not easily blend into the multi-layered structure that has produced the human conscience we know today with its accompanying sense of personal responsibility and moral restraint. How can a soldier in battle throw off six thousand years of this development without serious consequences? It is practically impossible to return to civilian life untainted by guilt and remorse, or by bitter cynicism. In contrast, primitive people considering themselves to be wholly agents of nature had no qualms about killing when called to arms. Failure in battle simply confirmed that the opposing force in a particular instance wielded greater power. Success in battle confirmed that the force within him was, in a particular instance, superior, and honor came to him for wielding the stronger force. But the outcome had no connection to the soul as it is understood today. The idea of free choice with its accompanying weight of personal responsibility did not enter his mind.

In one of his Essays, 'Of Honorary Awards,' the sixteenth-century essayist, Michel Eyquem de Montaigne, made some far-seeing observations on war and the human soul that would appear to counter the ideal soldier's need to tap into his aboriginal roots as related above. He said that a man who is able to survive the adversities in daily life should go to war with his whole soul because that soul will protect him from "the fear of death, of pain, and even of shame. Though a man may go to war out of duty alone, he will not have the contentment that a well-regulated conscience receives in itself for well-doing." [352] This fundamental truth no doubt accounted for the courage of the Viet Cong, and other indigenous armies of resistance against an invading force. For how can man's "well-regulated conscience" protect his soul if his heart and mind are not wedded to a cause that conforms to his conscience? The answer is that it cannot.

On the other hand, "fear of death, of pain, and even of shame," can be erased by other means. But not without a price. This was demonstrated by the protagonist in Stephen Crane's novel, *The Red Badge of Courage*. The trigger that inflamed Fleming, causing him to fight with fearless abandon, was the malignant swelling of a "wild hatred" for the enemy. In so far as his rage enabled him to overcome the enemy, it protected him physically. But had he taken to heart the abolitionists' cause, an equally powerful emotion would have conformed to his conscience and protected his soul. Henry never acquired human compassion for the suffering he saw among his comrades. He does not change from the day he joined up wanting to emulate the heroic way of life. His character does not mature or deepen. He is swelled by the fact that death did not touch him, that he had won over death and was therefore a hero. But, since military heroism and degradation coincide, Henry's future will be forever marked by the enduring presence of the beast. In like manner, personal hatred alone enabled many combatants of recent wars to survive. It was enough for an American soldier to have experienced one or more of his comrades' deaths for him to develop an all-consuming hatred for the enemy. One example of this occurred in Afghanistan's Korengal Valley to the men grieving for their lost comrade, Juan Restrepo. To rouse their passion before the next engagement, the platoon leader, Captain Kearney appealed to their instinct for revenge. He tells them, "Let's make the individuals who did this to us pay, let's make them feel like we do right now!"[353] With luck, the soldier rides this emotion to success, but there is a distinction between physical courage and genuine regard for others that constitutes moral courage. The combatant may physically survive without believing anything outside of hatred and revenge, but his soul has disappeared somewhere in the process, and he is never afterward at peace with his conscience.

Montaigne was writing and living as a recluse when the Religious Wars were ravaging sixteenth-century France. When the Bartholomew's Day massacre in 1572 unleashed Catholic violence against the Protestants, the power of sectarian passions affected him deeply. Although himself a Roman Catholic, it is impossible to imagine him supporting the Catholic prescription, for he was acting as a moderating influence respected by both the Catholic king and the king's Protestant brother-in-law, Henry of Navarre. In Montaigne's time, God's existence was a given, and the Roman Catholic Church, as the mouthpiece of God, was the guardian of the soul. In providing a safe harbor for the soul, its dogma became for many, an escape from personal responsibility. A devotee would not fear pain or death knowing that soul and duty were united in service to his religion. Montaigne must have realized that if the integrity of his soul should come in conflict with the authority of the church, duty alone was not enough to ward off fear in battle. The fact that he tried to negotiate with opposing factions in those wars, suggests that Montaigne's conscience was not at peace with the Catholic cause.

War Generates the Myth Upon Which It Feeds

Indeed, the idea of overcoming adversity and hardship has a religious significance that endures today. It was paramount in the chaplain's advice to Tim O'Brien during the Vietnam war. [354] The chaplain believed that war is good because it gives every fighting man a chance to show the strength of his soul. Fear of death, pain, or shame should not deter him from fighting no matter what a soldier may think about the reasons for a particular war. Why? Because war is a battle with death even more than with the opposing forces. How does obedience to a flag persuade a young soldier to desire a battle with death? It does because it appeals to all the "daring do" instincts of male youth. It has a neurological basis, and it is why some veterans actually miss the battlefield experience. It is why special forces like the Green Berets and the Navy Seals crave it. Poised between life and death, the intensity of that dark, terrifying sensation stimulates life itself. Should one lose that battle, the Christian promise of life beyond the grave for many will compensate the loss. Unfortunately, this makes the immediate cause of hostilities insignificant in comparison.

The willful offering up of life in the flower of youth and health is exceptional and shattering, whereas death as the biological end of a life well-lived attracts little attention beyond the grief of the family circle. In the Christian context, however, the personal confrontation with death is what matters. Pursued in battle, it is a subtle, but clear carrying forward of the ancient mindset. It raises man above anonymity and gives him the opportunity to show his mettle. Unfortunately, once undertaken, the tendency to prolong a war in order to justify past sacrifices even when victory is unobtainable, is irresistible. The result can only be more death and more wars in the future. In this way, the myth continues unabated, and it follows quite naturally that to honor young soldiers killed or wounded in combat, the ancient heroic ideal and the Christian symbol of sacrifice are prominently upheld in western military tradition. It is not surprising that a large photograph of five Marines carrying the Christian Cross to the top of a mountain at Camp Pendleton appeared on the front page of the Los Angeles Times in November of 2011. The action upholds the well-known symbol of death and suffering that underscores the cult of military heroism either institutionalized in war or individually undertaken. This is why the rationale for war is crucial since only through the power of a just and worthy cause—a cause that ultimately supports life in all its varied forms—can sacrifice be warranted. Otherwise, the Cross becomes wholly a symbol of death and destruction.

In any case, war should be undertaken only when all other avenues have been exhausted, the reason deeply felt by the combatant and embraced by the home front. When this occurs, death becomes a mere accident along the way because the cause is greater than the individual, and heroic status is not consciously sought. In the Christian context, however, the personal confrontation with death is what matters. Underwritten by the heroic ideal and the renown of the saints and martyrs rewarded in a mythical heaven, a believer is inclined to obey the call to arms regardless of the reason, for sacrifice must yield a return. In this context, death is less frightening, if not embraced. But for those who find themselves on the battlefield with neither the Christian faith nor a deeply felt cause, death is a calamity with all the recurring symptoms referred to in the preceding chapters.

CONCLUSION

After all the blood-spilling, nothing really has been accomplished that with intelligence and insight could have been resolved peacefully via diplomacy or perhaps avoided altogether. As Barbara Tuchman so aptly concluded about our involvement in Vietnam, "nothing was accomplished in the individual's interest, the national interest or in any other country's interest."[355] The U.S. had a complete absence of reflective thought about that undertaking, and she appears to be continuing in the same vein in the Middle East. Historical precedent might have anticipated the growing resentment of her own people for her meddling support of unpopular regimes. However mistakenly, the U.S. has inserted itself into Iraq, it behooves her to remain long enough to restore the social and economic void that resulted from the invasion. To simply walk away from a beaten down nation, is morally as well as strategically wrong. When thousands of Iraqi youths who had served with the U.S. military suddenly found themselves without jobs and a source of income, they were easy fodder for a budding ISIS. These foot-loose young men, many barely out of their teens, were easily recruited. The ideology has focused their anger and given them a way out of their present malaise. It has given them a cause: to unravel the boundaries artificially laid down after the First World War in the Treaty of Versailles and to reunite Iraq and Syria.[356]

While Americans publicly mourn the casualties among their own citizens (4,486 service members dead between 2003-2012, and 32,222 wounded),[357] Iraqi casualties have been hidden from view. Recently uncovered by Wikileaks, they are now in the open: 109,032 Iraqi deaths in total for the period 2004-2009 of which 66,081 were civilians and 23,000 enemy insurgents.

An additional 176,392 Iraqis have been seriously wounded. Since 2009, 15,000 dead and wounded have been added to the official count.[358] The first thing that hits the reader other than the total figure is the number of civilian casualties in proportion to enemy casualties. In fact, the number of civilians killed in Iraq exceeds the total number of American soldiers killed in the Vietnam War! As it did fifty years earlier to the Vietnamese, the cold calculations of the Defense Department have kept from the public the tragic consequences of this war on Iraqi families so as not to arouse compassion for the opposition and criticism of its own strategies. The Iraqi people will never give up demanding some kind of acknowledgment for their dead and wounded. It is hard to fathom how the U.S. can maintain its status as an innocent victim of terrorists' plots when its policies promote the very thing it fears.

The continuing U.S. collaboration with the unpopular government of Saudi Arabia is another precarious situation. When one considers that the men who highjacked U.S. planes in 2001 were Saudi members of al Qaeda, and that bin Laden was a Saudi national, it is difficult not to reach the conclusion that U.S. support of the Saudi family fueled the attack on the Trade Center.[359]

In his introduction to *Men at War*, Ernest Hemingway noted the prevalence of censorship during the war. It conceals "mistakes, blunders and acts of criminal misjudgment and negligence. These occur in all wars. But after the war is over, all of these acts have to be paid for." He goes on to say that "it is very easy to fool the people at the start of a war and run it on a confidential basis, but later the wounded start coming back and the actual news spreads.[360]

And the news is spreading. A war that is currently run on a confidential basis is the ongoing Saudi Arabia-led war in Yemen. It has killed thousands, forced millions to flee their homes, resulted in the world's worst cholera outbreak, and left seven million people at risk of starvation. It is fueled with American-made bombs, dropped by American-made planes, and refueled by American military forces. It has wreaked havoc on the people of Yemen. This confidential war is already stirring up a blow-back response among extremists in the Arabian Peninsula, fueling anti-American sentiment throughout Yemen and beyond, and certainly making the U.S. less safe. [361]

There was a feeling of Déjà Vu in former President Obama's commencement address at West Point on 28 May 2014. He reconfirmed the drawdown and withdrawal from Afghanistan.

Then, as if to reassure those who might infer a retreat from U.S. influence in foreign affairs, his National Security Advisor, Susan Rice, on the following day, confirmed that "the nation is prepared to act with force, if necessary, wherever on earth a threat to U.S. interests is eminent."[362] It remains to define just what and where U.S. interests lie, for, in addition to the consequences of using force to implement policy, there are economic repercussions. Three years later, the Inspector General for Reconstruction in Afghanistan revealed that the work so far has cost the American taxpayers 103 billion dollars, and that owing to corruption, fraud, and abuse in the Afghan government, much of that money has already been wasted, and the data to account for it is not available. [363]

Turning to Iran, an honest admission of U.S. accountability for the current state of affairs in that country might help the average person understand how anti-American sentiment builds into a blowback response. Iran's resentment toward the U.S. dates back to 1953, and the U.S. government's involvement in overthrowing their democratically elected Prime Minister Mohammed Mosaddegh in a CIA engineered Coup d'état and installing the unpopular, Shah Reza Pahlavi. Why? Because after years of the British/American-controlled oil companies profiting from Iranian oil at the expense of the Iranians, Mosaddegh, responding to a popular outcry for nationalizing the industry, was preparing to nationalize it. Today, Iran's intransigency toward U.S. efforts to negotiate a satisfactory nuclear nonproliferation treaty may find its source in unforgotten abuses of its autonomy by former American governments. This and other examples of the U.S. illegally meddling in other countries' affairs needs to come to light. It provides a sub-text for NSA Susan Rice's imprudent statement that the U.S. "is prepared to act with force, if necessary, wherever on earth a threat to U.S. interests is eminent."[364]

In his Nobel Lecture, Seamus Heaney stated that it was "difficult to repress the thought that history is about as instructive as an abattoir and that Tacitus was right to say that peace is merely the desolation left behind after the decisive operations of merciless power." [365] As writers and thinkers, we are wary of striking a positive note. Just as affairs between people are complicated, so the affairs of state and careful reflection should precede action. For in the haste to use force to solve what she perceives to be in her interest, the U.S. is in danger of growing evermore totalitarian, a direction that looms on the horizon of the newly elected Trump administration. Although President Obama genuinely believed that he was elected to get America off its war footing, he must have felt constrained to reassure a people whose self-esteem appears to rely on the need to advertise American exceptionalism far and wide and to intimidate those who would oppose her ambition. Because in his final State of the Union Address, he gushed, "The United States of America is the most powerful nation on earth. Period... Our troops are the finest fighting force in the history of the world. No nation dares to attack us or our allies because they know that's the path to ruin."[366] How far the U.S. means to go to live up to this reputation is the urgent issue of today.

In a recent article in the New Yorker, George Packer analyzes the first wave of literature coming from soldiers returning from Iraq. He perceptively compares the attitude of the public toward these soldiers with that of those coming back from Vietnam fifty years earlier. In contrast to the indifference shown by the Vietnam veterans, the soldiers returning from Iraq are widely celebrated as "heroes" appearing on the front pages of every local paper. "Both wars began with hubris and false victories, turned into prolonged stalemates, and finally deserved the bitter name of defeat." [367] How is it that a new generation of soldiers fighting in an unpopular war in which they have no stake outside themselves receive a hero's homecoming? Because, Packer explains, not having to endure a draft, today's public is emotionally disengaged with these new wars, and the fuss made over the soldiers who willingly volunteered, reflects a relationship that is embarrassingly false. Of course, much of this hype is a promotional pitch by the military itself to keep the ranks full and maintain a quota. *Thank You for Your Service* is the ironic title of one of these soldiers' books. "It captures all the bad faith of a civilian population that views itself as undeserving and the equivocal position of celebrated warriors who don't much feel like saying, "You're welcome." [368] Even though they return with all their illusions shattered, the fact that their initial desire to go to the edge regardless, confirms the staying power of those ancient myths now encased in clichés such as the belief that the military is where a person goes to become a man.

In a study of some 300 Vietnam veterans for The Nation in November 1982, Peter Marin was impressed by a particular kind of moral seriousness among them, "For them all conversation about human error or evil is a conversation about themselves; they are pushed past smug ideology and the condemnation of others to an examination of the world that is an examination of the human self. They know there is no easy relation between one's self-image and the consequences of one's actions." [369] On the battlefield, these veterans confronted the other side of the cross—their own capacity for evil. Stripped of the rationalizations that have camouflaged the brutality and excesses with patriotism and duty, the unvarnished truth revealed in the specific human actions recorded in the literature of that war has sobered and deepened these survivors. It is doubtful, however, that the American public will re-examine their country's self-image and its role on the world stage. The drive for profits by large weapons producers and advances in technology that gloss over the issues with the illusion that drones will solve the problem of fighting on the ground, keep American hubris alive. With each succeeding generation, the lessons of the past recede into history's dark corners. Every day the news is filled with seeds of new wars germinating.

EPILOGUE

In 2016, having finished the manuscript, my search for a publisher was disheartening. Vietnam was old news, was the common reply, a tragic loss to be buried in the history books of academia away from the eyes of future generations. Neither did it help that Alfredo Bonadeo was unable to dialogue with a publisher or anyone at all. But time does not stop, and events briefly touched upon in the final chapter of the book have darkly blossomed into endless conflicts that are repeating the missteps of an earlier time.

After twenty years of stalemate in Afghanistan, the outrage of the Vietnam venture re-appeared on the tarmac of the Afghan airport in September 2021. Watching the ensuing chaos unfold on TV and reading the news, one was unavoidably thrown into an atmosphere reminiscent of the hysteria in Da Nang and Saigon in April 1975.

Three months prior to the U. S. exit, National Security Analyst, Mark Thompson, presciently stated, "The U.S. is likely to end up losing its longest war, just as it ended up losing its previous longest war in Vietnam. The parallels are pertinent, and their lessons should be learned to keep the nation from making the same mistake a third time. Both wars bogged down because of support and supply lines beyond the borders of South Vietnam and exit from Afghanistan." He pointed to the U.S. refusal to take on a duplicitous Pakistan, the neighboring country whose government from the early years provided a "safe harbor" for bin Laden along with the Taliban and many Islamic extremists.[370]

But beyond the tactical failure above referenced, the central issue in any war is the cause and the combatants' belief in it. Forced to defend their land, against a foreign invader, the Taliban grew in number, gaining many sympathizers both inside and outside the country. Likewise, the North Vietnamese possessed a certainty resting on the belief that they were defending their country's independence and that their fight was just. They too had many sympathizers beyond their borders. In both wars, the battlefields were materially and spiritually connected to the insurgents. In both wars, uncommitted U.S. soldiers were alienated from military objectives and weighed down by an alien territory, language, and culture, and in both, many Vietnamese and Afghan combatants did not support their U.S.- backed governments. Neither the Diem regime nor President Ghani's National Defense & Security Forces could claim full support of their armies. Corruption in those governments and conflicting factions within each country bred a lack of motivation and lackluster military performance.

In sum, as Thompson stated, "The world's most powerful military was defeated . . . by a powerful Pashtun tribal insurgency." Correspondingly, I would add that fifty years ago, an army of tiny men, no bigger than boys, succeeded in driving out of their country a "race of giants."

HIDING THE TRUTH

Many military leaders were afraid to admit failure in Afghanistan. The public heard many times statements from top commanders that "we are turning the corner," or "overall our mission is on a positive trajectory." Retired Marine colonel, G. I. Wilson explained in 2011 why the generals would be reluctant, to tell the truth about Iraq and Afghanistan. He wrote, "Nurturing the Pentagon money flow and the domestic political environment that supports it while influencing their chosen successors to keep the money spigots open profoundly changes the message the retired generals and colonels send to the listening audience." [371] After all, many high officials look to retirement as board members of top Pentagon contractors such as Lockheed Martin, Raytheon, General Dynamics, Boeing, and Northrop Grumman. Additional service contracts that supported these wars went to the private contractors and their shareholders where approximately half the money the American people spent on the war went into the "coffers of defense contractors who either supplied weapons and equipment or provided services to support the war and reconstruction efforts."[372] This out-sourcing of jobs that in the past were performed by uniformed service members not only added to the cost but kept the revolving door revolving between corporate profit and military policy.

But service members within the ranks knew that the U.S. was fighting a lost cause. Afraid to speak publicly for fear of hurting their careers, it was apparent that dissent would not be tolerated lest it throw a monkey wrench into the lucrative partnership between the "tightly integrated web of defense contractors, military service bureaucracies, and politicians."[373]

And just what was the American cause? Bin Laden was found in Pakistan. Was it to transform Afghanistan or any other country for that matter, into a modern democracy? Was that the idea behind National Security Advisor, Susan Rice's statement that "the nation is prepared to act with force, if necessary, wherever on earth a threat to U.S. interests is imminent." Atty Gen. Eric Holder of the Obama Administration offered a definition of imminence that stretched common understandings of that word. In sum, his definition "suggests that if American forces have a fleeting chance to take a shot, the notion of imminence applies, even if a suspected attack might be months or years away."[374] Or, is the cause, what William M. Arkin states in *The Generals Have No Clothes,* to perpetuate the "gigantic physical superstructure" that sustains endless warfare," that is, the need to keep the ever-growing "apparatus of people, ships, bases, satellites, planes, drones, analysts, and contractors"[375] in business.

Lest the killing and maiming, of U.S. soldiers, and the destruction of cities and civilians in foreign wars, prick the consciences of U.S. authorities and the public, a new advance in technology has surfaced to allay the sting, namely, the use of drones and targeted airstrikes by remote piloted planes. Several presidential administrations have claimed that these airstrikes are an effective way to wage war while minimizing civilian casualties. (Note, there is no talk of changing U.S. policy to make war less likely.) But mounting evidence has appeared to contradict this claim. Imprecise targeting and flawed intelligence in the use of drones against ISIS have killed thousands of innocent civilians. More recently, a drone strike in Kabul in August 2021 killed 10 civilians and injured many more. These aggressive maneuvers are packaged as self- defensive measures against an imminent threat even though most have taken place hundreds of miles from the actual battlefield. The imminence is loosely applied, with self-defense as the new fiction that would justify a military attack. Worse: "This approach to war is a model that other countries are now following," wrote Christopher Faulkner, Andrew Stigler, and Jeffrey Rogg in a recent article in the LA Times. They give several examples of militant groups presently employing drones in civil conflicts including Mexican cartels in turf wars.

Drones and auto-piloted planes now keep American belligerency relatively hidden from the American public. This lulls people into the illusion that war is now more humane, and people can go about their business relatively undisturbed. But administrations continue to engage in foreign paramilitary operations most often thrusting American military might against small, weak nations currently in the Middle East. For this reason, Bonadeo has drawn on extensive literature from the Vietnam debacle to lay out in detail, the individual stories, the damage to body and soul, and the civilian lives destroyed. Abstract numbers fall vaguely on most people's ears. Fatality statistics given in the news, don't go to the heart of the readers about the individuals who comprise them. Whether it be more sophisticated weapons, traditional ground units, or clandestine machinations, the consequences are the same—anger from the other side provoking a crisis, blowback, and so more war.

To change the "pattern of arrogance and folly"—U.S. bases circling the globe ready to intervene whenever and wherever she feels her interests threatened—will take an act of humility, namely, the realization that her domestic problems—the climate crisis, gun violence, homelessness, health care, to name just a few that threaten her democracy—is where her true interests lie. They are profound and urgent.

Barbara Bonadeo, October 2022

ENDNOTES

Introduction
1. *Il piacere/Pleasure*, 1889; *Il trionfo della morte/The Triumph of Death*, 1894; *Il fuoco/The Flame of Life*, 1900; *Forse che si, forse che no/Maybe Yes, Maybe No*, 1910.
2. *Mussolini e la politica del sacrificio*, Aracne Press, Roma, 2009.
3. *Corruption, Conflict and Power in The Works and Times of Niccolo' Machiavelli* (University of California Press, 1973).

Chapter I. Due Cause
4. Karl von Clausewitz, *On War*, ed. and tr. M. Howard and P. Paret (Princeton 1984), pp. 76, 140, 187, 282.
5. Ibid, pp. 190,192
6. Stephen Crane, *The Red Badge of Courage*, ed H. Binder (New York, 1982), pp. 3,4, 6.
7. Ibid. pp 3,4,6.
8. Ibid, p.20.
9. Clausewitz, *On War*, pp. 76, 100, 140, 190-92, 282
10. Leo Tolstoy, *War and Peace*, tr. C. Garnett, New York, ed, pp. 752, 754.
11. Ibid, p. 752—754.
12. S.L.A. Marshall, *Men against Fire. The Problem of Battle Command*, Norman, 2000, pp. 161, 162.
13. Tim O'Brien, *The Things They Carried*, Broadway Books, 1990, pp. 40-41; O'Brien's interview in *Writing Vietnam, Writing Life*, ed. T. Herzog, Iowa City, 2008, p. 98.
14. William Westmoreland, *A Soldier Reports*, Da Capo Press, 1989, p. 423.
15. Bernard Fall, *Last Reflections on a War*, Double Day & Co, 1967, p. 175.
16. Tobey Herzog, *Writing Vietnam, Writing Life*, University of Iowa Press, pp. 24, 98-99: Caputo's and O'Brien's interviews.

17. Ronald Glasser, *365 Days,* George Braziller, N. Y., 1980, P.33.
18. John A. Parish, MD, 12, 20 & 5, *A Doctors Year in Vietnam,* E.P. Dutton & Co, 1972, p. 211.
19. Philip Caputo, *A Rumor of War,* Holt, Rinehart, Winston, 1972, PP xv, xvii, 191, 218-219.
20. O'Brien, *Going After Cacciato,* Dell, 1978. pp 320-21.
21. O'Brien, *The Things They Carried,* Broadway Books, New York, p 21.
22. O'Brien, *Going After Cacciato,* p 238, 240.
23. Al Santoli, *Everything We Had. An Oral History of the Vietnam War by Thirty-three American Soldiers Who Fought It,* Random House, New York, 1981, pp. 68-69.
24. W. D. Ehrhart, *Vietnam—Perkasie. A Combat Marine Memoir* (London, 1983), p. 2. A further account of the wide-spread war crimes committed by Americans in Vietnam, is found in *Kill Anything That Moves, The Real American War in Vietnam,* by Nick Turse, (Henry Holt & Co. New York, 2013).
25. *Dear America. Letters Home from Vietnam,* ed. B. Edelman (New York,1985), p. 66
26. James Webb, *Fields of Fire,* Prentice Hall, (Englewood Cliffs, 1978), p. 168.
27. William Broyles, *Brothers in Arms. A Journey from War to Peace,* Knopf, (New York, 1986), pp. 22, 91, 136, 198, 200, 235.
28. Fall, *Last Reflections on a War,* p. 189, 254.
29. Ibid, 189.
30. Walter Capps, *The Unfinished War,* Beacon Press, (Boston, 1982) pp. 59-60.
31. Michael Shafer, "The Vietnam Combat Experience: The Human Legacy," in *The Vietnam War in the American Imagination,* Beacon Press, 1990, p. 84.
32. O'Brien, *Going After Cacciato,* p. 318.
33. Ward Just, *To What End,* Boston: Houghton Mifflin, 1968, p. 77.
34. Harry Summers, *On Strategy, A Critical Analysis of the Vietnam War,* Novato, 1982, pp. 96, 176.
35. Ibid. pp. 34-35.
36. Just, *To What End,* pp. 24-25.
37. Theodore Draper, *Abuse of Power,* Viking, New York, 1967, pp. 161-62.
38. Fredrik Logevall, *Choosing War. The Lost Chance for Peace and the Escalation of War in Vietnam,* U. of California Press, Berkeley, 1999, p. 385.
39. Robert McNamara, *In Retrospect. The Tragedy and Lessons of Vietnam,* Vintage Books, 1996, p. 309
40. David Halberstam, *The Best and the Brightest,* Random House, 1972, pp, 328,541.

41. *The Memoirs of Richard Nixon*, Grosset & Dunlap, 1978, pp. 257, 269.
42. Broyles, *Brothers in Arms*, p. 99.
43. Fall, *Last Reflections on a War*, p. 286.
44. Stanley Karnow, *Vietnam. A History,* Penguin, New York, 1983, p. 438.
45. Norman Podhoretz, *Why We Were in Vietnam,* (New York, 1982), pp. 107, 197.
46. Karnow, *Vietnam, A History*, p. 169.
47. Ibid, pp. 250, 326.
48. Westmoreland, *A Soldier Reports*, p. 423.
49. William Calley, *Body Count* (London, 1971), p. 132.
50. Karnow, *Vietnam*, p. 253.
51. Westmoreland, *A Soldier Reports*, p. 362.
52. Logevall, *The Lost Chance for Peace and the Escalation of War in Vietnam*, pp. 356, 357.
53. *The Memoirs of Richard Nixon*, p. 271.
54. Westmoreland, *A Soldier Reports*, p. 402.
55. Robin Moore, *The Green Berets,* Crown, New York, 1965, pp. 70, 158-59, 348.
56. Harold Moore and Joseph Galloway, *We Were Soldiers Once... and Young,* (New York, 2002), pp. 2, 117, 133, 203, 214.
57. Webb, *Fields of Fire*, p. 28.
58. O'Brien, *Going After Cacciato,* pp. 197-98, 201
59. McNamara, *In Retrospect*, pp. 322-23.
60. Lewis Puller, Jr., *Fortunate Son*, Grove Press, New York, 1991, p.234.
61. Broyles, *Brothers in Arms*, p. 137.
62. Glasser, *365 Days*, p. 34.
63. Michael Charlton and Anthony Moncrieff, *Many Reasons Why*, The American Involvement in Vietnam, Hill and Wang, New York, 1978, p.137.
64. Charles Anderson, *The Grunts*, Presidio Press, San Rafael, 1983, p. 167.
65. Note: U.S. involvement in Vietnam unfolded against the domestic backdrop of the civil rights movement whose leaders and other critics described the conflict as racist—"a white man's war, a black man's fight." Because Selective Service regulations offered deferments for college attendance and some civilian occupations that favored middle and upper -class whites, the reality of the time struck hard on the African American community. Although Black Americans did supply a large number of troops, a high percentage of these had voluntarily enlisted. African Americans made up roughly only 12 percent of the Army and Marine total (in line with national population figures) yet, they frequently contributed half the men in front-line combat units.

66. Ron Kovic, *Born on the Fourth of July*, Pocket Books, 1976, New York, pp. 54-55, 63, 73.
67. Ibid, pp. 218-19, 222.
68. Puller, *Fortunate Son*, pp. 30, 33, 156-58.
69. Ibid., pp. 234, 253, 260, 279.
70. Caputo, *A Rumor of War*, pp. xiv, 5, 6, 66, 182.
71. "Ambush" by James McLeroy, *Dear America, Letters Home from Vietnam*, p. 66.
72. Ibid, p. 16, 217.
73. Webb, *Fields of Fire,* An anonymous general to correspondent Arthur Hadley, p.1.
74. Kovic, *Born on the Fourth of July*, p.166.
75. O'Brien, *Going after Cacciato*, p. 62.
76. Tobey Herzog, *Writing Vietnam, Writing Life*, Univ. of Iowa Press, Larry Heinemann's interview; p. 72.
77. Ibid, O'Brien's interview, pp. 98-99.
78. Caputo, *A Rumor of War*, pp. 77, 89.
79. Ibid. pp. 93, 98
80. O'Brien, *The Things They Carried*, p. 15.
81. Anderson, *The Grunts*, p. 58.
82. Caputo, *A Rumor of War*, pp. 100, 272-73.
83. Larry Heinemann, *Close Quarters*, Farrar, Straus, Giroux, New York, 1977, p. 19.
84. Robert Mason, *Chickenhawk,* Penguin, New York, 1985), p. 440.
85. Michael Herr, *Dispatches,* Avon, New York, 1978), p. 59.
86. McNamara *In Retrospect*, p. 333.
87. Anderson, *The Grunts*, pp. 193, 200.
88. Neil Sheehan, *The Bright Shining Lie, John Paul Vann and America in Vietnam*, Random House, New York, 1988, p. 741.
89. Marshall, *Men Against Fire*, University of Oklahoma Press, Norman, 2000, pp. 161, 162.

Chapter II. Killing

90. Gustav Hasford, *The Short-Timers*, Harper and Row, New Work, 1979, p. 136.
91. Michael Herr, *Dispatches*, Avon Books, New York, 1968, p. 20.
92. Webb, *Fields of Fire*, p. 223.
93. Summers, *On Strategy*, p. 33.
94. O'Brien, *The Things They Carried*, p. 200.
95. Caputo, *A Rumor of War*, pp. 306, 309.
96. Herr, *Dispatches*, p. 103

97 Caputo, *A Rumor of War*, p. 219.
98 Herr, *Dispatches*, pp. 5-6.
99 Robert J Lifton, *Home from the War*, Simon & Shuster, New York; p. 59-60.
100 Heinemann, *Close Quarters*, p. 73.
101 O'Brien, *If I Die in a Combat Zone*, pp. 76, 79.
102 Herr, *Dispatches*, p. 179.
103 Puller, *Fortunate Son*, p. 80.
104 Herr, *Dispatches*, p. 19.
105 Anderson, *The Grunts*, pp. 121-23.
106 Webb, *Fields of Fire*, pp. 135-36, 291.
107 Santoli, *Everything We Had*, p. 148.
108 Caputo, *A Rumor of War*, p. 251.
109 O'Brien, *If I Die in a Combat Zone*, p. 130.
110 Caputo, *A Rumor of War*, pp. xvi, xvii, 218, 251, 252.
111 Hasford, *Short-Timers*, p. 84.
112 Herr, *Dispatches*, pp. 63, 66.
113 Caputo, *A Rumor of War*, 287-89.
114 Ibid, pp. 277-78.
115 Herr, *Dispatches*, pp. 58-59.
116 *Dear America*, pp. 94, 95.
117 Herr, *Dispatches*, p. 58
118 Wallace Terry, *Bloods, An Oral History of the Vietnam War by Black Veterans*, Random House, (New York, 1984), p.13.
119 Santoli, *Everything We Had*, p. 212.
120 Jonathan Shay, *Achilles in Vietnam Combat Trauma and the Undoing of Character*, Simon & Shuster, (New York, 1995), pp. 78, 95, 96.
121 Ibid., pp. 84, 201.
122 Herr, *Dispatches*, pp. 198-99.
123 Webb, *Fields of Fire*, p. 336.
124 Herr, *Dispatches*, p, 62.
125 Broyles, *Brothers in Arms*, p. 201.
126 *Nam, The Vietnam War in the Words of the Men and Women Who Fought There*, ed. M. Baker, William Morrow, (New York, 1981), p. 166.
127 Fall, *Street without Joy*, Mechanicsburg, 2005, p. 373.
128 Broyles, *Brothers in Arms*, pp. 200, 201.
129 Santoli, *Everything We Had*, p.49`.
130 O'Brien, *Going after Cacciato*, pp. 125, 131; Id., In the Lake of the Woods (New York, 1995), pp. 104, 203.

131 *Dear America*, p. 70.
132 Ibid., p. 50.
133 Lifton, *Home from the War*, p. 59.
134 Broyles, *Brothers in Arms*, p. 270.
135 Ibid., p. 5.
136 O'Brien, *Going after Cacciato*, pp. 309, 310.
137 Daniel Lang, *Casualties of War*, New York, 1969, pp. 19-20.
138 Anderson, *The Grunts*, pp. 179-80, 184
139 *Dear America*, p. 62
140 Podhoretz, *Why We Were in Vietnam*, p. 185.
141 Ward Just, *To What End*, Boston 1968, p. 165.
142 *Nam*, pp. 63-64.
143 Ibid pp 63,64
144 Glasser, *365 Days*, p. 34.
145 David Hackworth & Julie Sherman, *About Face*, The Odyssey of an American Warrior, Simon & Shuster, pp. 572, 778.
146 Herr, *Dispatches*, p. 172.
147 Westmoreland, *A Soldier Reports*, p. 273.
148 Lifton, *Home from the War*, pp. 64, 65.
149 Robert Roth, *Sand in the Wind* Hackworth, Little Brown & Co. 1973, p.79. Dave Grossman, *On Killing, The Psychological Cost of Learning to Kill in War and Society*, New York 1996, p. 252.
150 Caputo, *A Rumor of War*, pp. 34-35.
151 Richard Hammer, *The Court-Martial of Lt. Calley*, Coward, McCann & Geoghegan, Inc. 1971, p. 158.
152 *Nam*, p. 56-57.
153 Caputo, *A Rumor of War*, p. 164.
154 Ibid. p. xvii
155 Loren Baritz, *Backfire*, New York, 1986, p.290.
156 Caputo, *A Rumor of War*, 294
157 Ibid, p. 129.
158 Ibid, p. 11.
159 Lifton *Home from the War*, pp. 45, 64.
160 Ibid, p. 36.
161 Ibid, p. 50.
162 Seymour Hersh, *My Lai 4*, A Report on the Massacre and its Aftermath, New York, 1970, p. 42.
163 Hammer, *The Court-Martial of Lt. Calley*, p. 263.

164 Lifton, *Home from the War*, p. 55.
165 Hammer, *The Court-Martial of Lt. Calley*, pp. 158,159.
166 Lifton, *Home from the War*, p. 60.
167 Hammer, *The Court-Martial of Lt. Calley*, pp. 258, 274-275.
168 Hersh, *My Lai 4*, pp. 33, 40-42.
169 Hammer, *The Court-Martial of Lt. Calley*, pp. 4, 6, 258.
170 *Nam*, 171.
171 Nick Turse, *Kill Anything That Moves*, Picador, New York, 2013, p.5.
172 Hammer, *The Court-Martial of Lt. Calley*, pp. 3,4, 6.
173 Hersh, *My Lai 4*, p. 80.
174 Lifton, *Home from the War*, p. 56.
175 Anderson, *The Grunts*, p. 201
176 Caputo, *A Rumor of War*, pp. xvii.
177 *Dear America*, p. 118.
178 Webb, *Fields of Fire*, pp. 223-24.
179 Calley, *Body Count*, pp. 124-125.
180 Wilson, *The LBJ Brigade*, p. 56.
181 Moore and Galloway, *We Were Soldiers Once... and Young*, pp. 214, 218, 373-74, 408, 445.)
182 Peter Cowie, *The Apocalypse Now* (Da Capo Press, 2001).
183 Moore and Galloway, *We Were Soldiers Once ... and Young*, pp. 80, 92, 93, 94, 98, 99, 106, 107, 109, 114, 206, 208, 214.
184 Ibid, 442-43
185 Herr, *Dispatches*, p. 257.
186 Robin Moore, *The Green Berets*, Crown, New York, pp. 170-171, 203.
187 Ibid., p. 348.
188 Grossman, *On Killing*, pp. 291-93.
189 Fall, *Last Reflections on a War*, p. 252.
190 Heinemann, *Close Quarters*, pp. 278-81
191 O'Brien, *The Things They Carried*, pp. 124, 125, 127, 128, 134.

III. Dying

192 "Obituary for Paul Fussell," The Economist, June 9, 2012.
193 Harry G. Summers, Jr., *On Strategy*, Presidio Press, CA, p.33.
194 Bernard Fall, *Last Reflections on a War*, N.Y. 1968.
195 Webb, *Fields of Fire*, p. 166.
196 Glenn Gray, *The Warriors, Reflections on Men in Battle*, Harper & Row, 1970, p.116.

197. Robert J Lifton, *Home from the War*, p. 99.
198. O'Brien, *Going after Cacciato*, p. 13.
199. Herr, *Dispatches*, p. 71.
200. Caputo, *A Rumor of War*, pp. 164, 165.
201. Herr, *Dispatches*, pp. 12, 14.
202. Caputo, *A Rumor of War*, p. 80.
203. Hasford, *Short-Timers*, p. 129.
204. Herr, *Dispatches*, p. 66.
205. Caputo, *A Rumor of War*, pp. 57, 93.
206. David Halberstam, *One Very Hot Day*, Houghton Mifflin Co. Boston, 1967, p. 81.
207. Stephen Wright, *Meditations in Green*, Scribner's Sons, 1983, pp. 153, 157-58.
208. Caputo, *A Rumor of War*, pp. 92, 100.
209. Webb, *Fields of Fire*, pp. 59, 187.
210. Anderson, *The Grunts*, pp. 54-55.
211. Ibid, p. 145.
212. Caputo, *A Rumor of War*, p. 121.
213. O'Brien, *The Things They Carried*, pp. 242-43.
214. Anderson, *The Grunts*, p. 134.
215. Caputo, *A Rumor of War*, p. 161.
216. Heinemann, *Close Quarters*, p. 252.
217. Ibid, p. 13.
218. O'Brien, *The Things they Carried*, pp. 20, 21, 238.
219. Mason, *Chickenhawk*, pp. 451-52, 455.
220. Caputo, *A Rumor of War*, pp. 246-48, 258.
221. Webb, *Fields of Fire*, p. 262.
222. Herr, *Dispatches*, p. 87.
223. Hasford, *Short-Timers*, p. 151.
224. O'Brien, *The Things They Carried*, p. 21.
225. Caputo, *A Rumor of War*, p. 90.
226. Herr, *Dispatches*, pp. 133-34.
227. Caputo, *A Rumor of War*, p. 273.
228. O'Brien, *If I Die in a Combat Zone*, p. 130.
229. Heinemann, *Close Quarters*, p. 45.
230. O'Brien, *If I Die in a Combat Zone*, p. 141.
231. Herr, *Dispatches*, p. 63.
232. O'Brien, *If I Die in a Combat Zone*, p. 106.
233. Caputo, *A Rumor of War*, pp. 277-78.
234. Mason, *Chickenhawk*, pp. 220-21.
235. Santoli, *Everything We Had*, pp. 177.

236 Mason, *Chickenhawk*, pp. 212, 218, 221, 228.
237 Ibid., *Chickenhawk*, pp. 212, 243, 279.
238 Malcolm Browne, *The New Face of War,* Bantam, 1986, p. 82.
239 Westmoreland, *A Soldier Reports*, pp. 83, 152, 153.
240 David Hackworth, *About Face, the Odyssey of an American Warrior*, Simon & Schuster, 1989, p. 498.
241 Moore and Galloway, *We Were Soldiers Once ... and Young*, pp. 439-40.
242 Caputo, *A Rumor of War*, p. 169.
243 Santoli, *Everything We Had*, pp. 72-73
244 Anderson, *The Grunts*, pp. 72-73.
245 Westmoreland, *A Soldier Reports*, p. 299.
246 Webb, *Fields of Fire*, p. 99.
247 Caputo, *A Rumor of War*, pp. 214-15.
248 Edelman, *Dear America, Letters Home from Vietnam*, p. 99.
249 Herr, *Dispatches*, pp. 143, 145, 149, 150, 163.
250 Webb, *Fields of Fire*, pp. 135-36.
251 Caputo, *A Rumor of War*, p. 169.
252 Gray, *The Warriors*, p. 128.
253 Moore and Galloway, *We Were Soldiers Once... and Young*, pp. 442-43.
254 Broyles, *Brothers in Arms*, pp. 80, 81, 200.
255 Quoted by Ernest Simmons, *Leo Tolstoy, The Years of Development*, 1828-1879, New York   1960, p.125.
256 Herr, *Dispatches*, pp. 102-03.
257 Broyles, *Brothers in Arms*, pp. 200, 267.
258 Ibid., p. 91.
259 Henry Kissinger, *Diplomacy,* Simon & Shuster, (New York, 1994), p. 660.
260 Hackworth, *About Face,* p. 698.
261 David Halberstam, *The Best and the Brightest*, Random House, 1972, p. 613.
262 Broyles, *Brothers in Arms*, p. 22.
263 O'Brien, *If I Die in a Combat Zone*, p. 57.
264 O'Brien, *Going After Cacciato*, pp. 201-03.
265 Ibid, p. 62.
266 O'Brien, *The Things They Carried*, p. 223.
267 Lifton, *Home from the War*, p. 222-23.
268 Caputo, *A Rumor of War*, p. 196.
269 Herr, *Dispatches*, p. 9.
270 From a poem titled "Ambush" (1967) in *Dear America*, p. 66.
271 Caputo, *A Rumor of War*, pp. 190, 191.
272 Kovic, *Born on the Fourth of July*, pp. 218-19, 221-22.

273 Caputo, *A Rumor of War*, pp. 5, 6, 14.
274 Ibid., pp. xv, 191.
275 Puller, *Fortunate Son*, pp. 276, 279.
276 Herr, *Dispatches*, pp. 9, 16.
277 *Dear America, Letters Home from Vietnam*, p. 80.
278 Herr, *Dispatches*, p. 87.
279 O'Brien, *If I Die in a Combat Zone*, p. 136; Caputo, *A Rumor of War*, p. 222.
280 Caputo, *A Rumor of War*, pp. 209-10.
281 Ibid., pp. 153-54.
282 Ibid., pp. 153, 212-13; Santoli, *Everything We Had*, pp. 108-09
283 O'Brien, *The Things They Carried*, pp. 149, 159, 165, 171, 184-85.
284 Caputo, *A Rumor of War*, pp. 121, 170.
285 See for instance E. B. Sledge, *With the Old Breed at Peleliu and Okinawa* (New York, 1990).
286 Herr, *Dispatches*, p.103.
287 O'Brien, *If I Die in a Combat Zone*, pp. 167-68.
288 Herr, *Dispatches*, p. 103.
289 Broyles, *Brothers in Arms*, p. 254.
290 Caputo, *A Rumor of War*, pp. XIV, XIX.
291 Anderson, *The Grunts*, p. 201.
292 O'Brien, *If I Die in a Combat Zone*, pp. 135-36.
293 William Wilson, *The LBJ Brigade*, Apocalypse Corp., CA, 1966, pp. 11, 56.
294 Caputo, *A Rumor of War*, p. 217.
295 Webb, *Fields of Fires*, p. 187.
296 Caputo, *A Rumor of War*, pp. xvii, 320.
297 Sabastian Junger, Ted Salon transcript, New York 2014
298 Regarding the "The paradox that inescapable defeat with its approach toward death, may bring us close to grasping something essential that eludes us in the ordinary events of life." David Morris (*The Culture of Pain*, Berkeley, 1991) sites Joyce Carol Oates who in her essay on boxing "sees boxing as a self-destructive pursuit that the boxer cannot avoid because avoiding pain means avoiding the exaltation that lifts him above the plane of everyday life."
299 O'Brien, *The Things They Carried*, pp. 81, 192, 238-39, 244.
300 Junger, Sabastian, TED Salon, New York, 2014.
301 Jeremy Scahill, *Dirty Wars*, Nation Books, New York, 2013, pp. 448, 449.
302 O'Brien, *The Things They Carried*, pp. 81, 175.
303 Heinemann, *Paco's Story*, (New York, 1987), p. 46; Id., *Close Quarters*, p. 163.

IV. The Legacy

304 Chelsea Manning, August 22, 2013
305 Bernard Fall, *Last Reflections on a War*, p. 189.
306 Walter Capps, *The Unfinished War*, p.59
307 Shay, *Achilles in Vietnam,* Touchtone, 1994, p. 114
308 Susan Sontag, *At the Same Time*, Essays and Speeches, Farrar, Straus, & Giroux, 2007.
309 Andrew J. Bacevich, "Baghdad Meets Saigon," Los Angeles Times, 6/15/14.
310 Natasha Bantwal for Facts of the Vietnam War, html.
311 McNamara, *In Retrospect*, p. 333.
312 USA Today Special Edition, "Vietnamese War Veterans Share Their Experiences with American Students."
313 United States and the Security Council, Frederking.
314 D. Frantz, "A Nation Challenged. The Afghans: The Taliban Wants to Negotiate with the U.S. Over bin Laden," New York Times, October 3, 2001.
315 "Diplomats Meet with Taliban on bin Laden: Some Contend U.S. Missed its Chance," Washington Post, October 29, 2001.
316 "Foreign Fighters of Harsher Bent Bolster the Taliban," New York Times, October 30, 2007.
317 Los Angeles Times, Op-Ed, January 12, 2014.
318 Los Angeles Times, October 22, 2011.
319 Ibid, January 12, 2012
320 Barbara Tuchman, *The March of Folly, From Troy to Vietnam*, Knopf, 1984, p. 307.
321 *Restrepo*, One Platoon, One Valley One Year, National Geographic, 2010.
322 Scahill, *Dirty Wars*, p. 329, 333.
323 Ibid, p. 346.
324 "Underneath the Armor," Elliott D. Woods; The Sun, March 2012.
325 Los Angeles Times, 1/13/12
326 Herr, *Dispatches*, pp 198, 199.
327 Santa Barbara News-Press, 3/13/2012
328 Santa Barbara News-Press, March 17, 2012.
329 Los Angeles Times, March 17, 2012.
330 The Defense Monitor: "Purge the Generals, What it Will Take to Fix the Army," Lieutenant Col. Daniel Davis, July-October, 2013.
331 Truthdig Reports: "Murder is Not an Anomaly in War," Chris Hedges, 3/19/12

332. Sundance. Documentary on Afghanistan. Since the film, there has been news of a successful uprising among the villagers in Zangabad. LA Times, 6/2/2013.
333. Shay, *Achilles in Vietnam*, p.78
334. Ibid. p. 5.
335. Steven Elliott, "Enduring Guilt," The Shooter Who Fired in Tillman's Direction.
336. Major Thomas' speech in a review by Leah Krevit of the film, Breaker Morant.
337. The Santa Barbara News-Press, 1/18/2012.
338. Quoted in an essay by William J. Astore. The Santa Barbara News Press.
339. The Santa Barbara News-Press, 1/18/2012
340. Los Angeles Times, 9/15/11.
341. The Boston Globe, 11/11/11
342. Heinemann, *Close Quarters*, (N.Y. 1977), pp 311, 312
343. Such military conduct has been a violation of all protocols established by the Geneva Conventions, the Hague Conventions, and the rules of military conduct laid down through institutions such as the United Nations or the International Criminal Court. Nothing has been capable of restraining the human rights violations that accompany modern warfare.
344. New York Times, 12/15/11
345. Los Angeles Times, 1/12/2012
346. William J. Astore, "The Harm in Hero Worship," Santa Barbara News-Press
347. Ibid.
348. Claude Levi-Strauss, *The Savage Mind*, Chicago, 1966, p. 219.
349. James G. Frazer, *The Golden Bough*, Macmillan Co.1969, Chapt. IV. Robert Graves, *The White Goddess*, Farrar, Straus, and Giroux, 1966.
350. Homer's *Iliad,* trans. Alexander Pope, Book XXIV.
351. Euripides II, *Heracles*, trans. William Arrowsmith, Chicago 1956, 965,1425.
352. Bonadeo, "Montaigne and War," Journal of the History of Ideas, July-September, 1985.
353. *Restrepo*, One Platoon, One Valley, One Year. 2007.
354. O'Brien, *If I Die In A Combat Zone*, pp. 56, 57
355. Tuchman, *The March of Folly from Troy to Vietnam*, P. 376.
356. After World War I, the European powers divided up the region formerly ruled by the Ottomans Syria and Lebanon became a French protectorate. Iraq, Transjordan and Palestine came under control of the British. The Arabian Peninsula was given to the Saudi family who created the Kingdom of Saudi Arabia in 1932. According to British historian, James Barr, two European colonial powers, Britain and France, literally drew "lines in the

sand," and to satisfy their own needs, constructed a map that completely disregarded ethno-religious realities.

357 Wikipedia, The Free Encyclopedia: U.S. Military Casualties of War, Iraq, 2003-2011.

358 The Guardian.com/news/datablog/2010/wikileaks-Iraq-data-journalism. The remaining 18,967 casualties fall between coalition forces and Iraqi government forces.

359 In Saudi Arabia, Human Rights groups have long criticized violations by the Saudi family. At present, these groups are alarmed over US military assistance in the Saudi bombing of Yemen that in 2015 had killed over 3,000 civilians, and as of this writing, continues unabated.

360 *Men at War, The Best War Stories of All Time*, edited by Ernest Hemingway, Bramhall House, 1955

361 "Win Without War:" The Center for International Policy; Washington, D.C., September, 2017.

362 President Obama's speech at West Point as reported in the Guardian May 28, 2014. Charlie Rose's interview of Susan Rice on PBS, May 29, 2014.

363 John Sopko, Special Inspector General for Afghanistan Reconstruction. Progress Report Hearing, November 1, 2017.

364 Charlie Rose's interview of Susan Rice on PBS, May 29, 2014.

365 Seamus Heaney, *Crediting Poetry*, The Nobel Lecture, Farrar Straus Giroux, 1995, p. 27.

366 President Obama's State of the Union Address, January, 2016.

367 George Packer, *Home Fires*, How Soldiers Write Their Wars, The New Yorker, April 7, 2014.

368 Ibid.

369 Peter Marin, The Nation, November 27, 1982.

370 Mark Thompson, The Key Reason the U.S. Lost in Afghanistan, The Defense Monitor, April-June 2021.

371 Dan Grazier, Afghanistan Proved Eisenhower Correct, The Defense Monitor, Oct-Dec, 2021.

372 Ibid, p. 3

373 Ibid, p. 3

374 Faulkner, Stigler, and Rogg, U.S. Airstrikes Fuel Reckless War, Los Angeles Times, 1/23/22.

375 William M. Arkin, *The Generals Have No Clothes*, (Simon & Schuster); The New Yorker, 9/13/21.

INDEX

A

Afghanistan xvii, xviii, xix, 97, 99, 104, 106, 107, 108, 109, 111, 112, 113, 121, 127, 131, 132, 133
Amerson, Thomas 111
Arkin, William M. 133
Astore, William 117

B

Bacevich, Andrew 101, 105
Bartholomew's Day Massacre 122
Berets, Green 12, 54, 55, 56, 120, 123
Bernard Fall 7, 57, 60, 99
Bien Phu, Dien 42, 80, 99
Bin Laden, Osama 97, 104
Blowback 105, 127, 134
Body Count 4, 25, 26, 45, 46, 47, 49, 50, 51, 84, 97
Bohlinger 110
Borodino, Battle of 3
Bravo Company 66
Bronze Age 118
Broyles 15, 16, 39, 41, 81
Bush xvii, 105, 106

C

Calley, William 46, 48, 49, 50, 52, 113
Camp Pendleton 123
Captain Kearney 107, 122
Captain Rhallon 5
Caputo, Philip 5, 18, 88
Cardinal Spellman, Francis 100
Checkerboard 76, 77
Chinese Premier Jiang Zemin 103
Christopher Faulkner, Andrew Stigler, and Jeffrey Rogg 134
Clausewitz, Karl von 1
Combat Assault 53, 73, 74
Communism 10, 11, 13, 15, 19, 22, 23, 29, 55, 88, 100
Cong, Viet 7, 10, 17, 22, 27, 28, 30, 37, 39, 40, 41, 42, 43, 44, 45, 47, 49, 53, 59, 60, 65, 76, 77, 78, 83, 84, 96, 102, 103, 121
Coppola, Francis 40
Cordillera, Annamese 21
Crane, Stephen xiii, xiv, 1, 121

D

Defense Monitor 111
Diem, Ngo Dinh 4, 100, 107
Drones 129, 133, 134

E

Elliott, Steven 113
Excalibur 40

F

Fussell, Paul 59

G

Gardez, province of 107
General James Amos 110
General McChrystal 108
Gilgamesh 120
Going Berserk 35, 37
Guadalcanal 78, 88

H

Haditha, Iraq 110
Halberstam 65
Heaney, Seamus 127
Hedges, Chris 112
Heinemann, Larry 57, 115
Hemingway, Ernest 126
Henry Cabot Lodge 10
Hercules 119
Ho Chi Minh 4, 11
Holder, Eric 133
Hussein, Saddam 105

I

Ia Drang Valley 28, 74, 75
Iran 127

Iraqi 107, 110, 116, 125, 126
ISIS 125, 133

J

Johnson, Chalmers 105
Junger, Sabastian 97

K

Kabul 104, 112, 134
Kandahar 111, 112
Kissinger, Henry 83
Korengal Valley 107, 121
Kovic 16, 17, 18, 20, 87

L

Lai, My xvi, xvii, xviii, 48, 49, 50, 51, 52, 111
Levi-Strauss, Claude 118

M

Marin, Peter 129
Marines 39, 46, 47, 63, 64, 69, 70, 78, 79, 81, 82, 88, 95, 109, 110, 111, 123
McNamara 15, 23, 102
Menand, Louis 114
Montaigne 121, 122
Moore, Robin 12, 54, 55
Morant, Breaker 113

N

Nam 16, 95
Nang, Da 36, 131
Napoleon 3
National Liberation Front 4
Navy Seals 37, 97, 109, 120, 123

Newspeak 27
Nixon, Richard 10, 12

O

O'Brien, Tim xvi, 3, 58, 92, 122

P

Packer, George 128
Pakistan 104, 131, 133
Persian Gulf War 103, 105
Pleiku 75
President Ghani 132
President Johnson 8, 10, 11, 99,
President Karzai 107
President Musharraf 104
President Obama 97, 108, 127, 128
Prime Minister Mohammed Mosaddegh 127
PTSD xviii
Puller, Lewis 15

Q

Qaeda, Al 104, 105, 106, 108, 126

R

Restrepo, Juan 122
Reza Pahlavi, Shah 127
Rice, Susan 127, 133
Romney, Mitt 106
Rusk, Dean 9, 10

S

S.L.A. Marshall 3, 24
Saigon 24, 59, 131

Sanh, Khe 28, 71, 79, 80, 89
Saudi Arabia 126
Search and Destroy 4, 20, 21, 44, 45, 49, 65, 69, 76, 77, 78, 80
Song Tra Bong River 41
Sontag, Susan 100
Suicide xix, 5, 18, 69, 86, 87, 88, 114, 115
Summers 8, 61

T

Taliban 104, 105, 106, 107, 108, 109, 112, 131, 132
Thompson, Mark 131
Tillman, Pat 113
Tolstoy xiii, 2, 3, 82,
Treaty of Versailles 125
Tuchman, Barbara 125

W

Weinberger doctrine 56
Westmoreland 3, 4, 8, 11, 12, 16, 24, 46, 50, 60, 62, 63, 76, 77, 80
Wilson, G.I. 132
Woods, Elliott 109

Y

Yemen 126, 127

Z

Zaeef, Abdaul Salam 104

www.ingramcontent.com/pod-product-compliance
Lightning Source LLC
LaVergne TN
LVHW041813060526
838201LV00046B/1248